Ports,
Prosthetics,
and a Whole Lotta
Prayer

A HOPEFUL MEMOIR OF A MOTHER'S
FIERCE LOVE IN THE DARKEST OF TIMES

Ports,
Prosthetics,
and a Whole Lotta
Prayer

ASHLEY SELBY-KARNEY

Ports, Prosthetics, and a Whole Lotta Prayer: A Hopeful Memoir of a Mother's Fierce Love in the Darkest of Times
Ashley Selby-Karney

Published by Leave Your Mark
PO Box 364
Yantis, TX 75497

Cover design: Kent Jensen | knail.com
Interior design and typesetting: Bel Esprit Books

ISBN: 979-8-9940386-3-5

First Edition: January 2026

CONTENTS

God is transforming your pain into something purposeful and beautiful.

INTRODUCTION

IN MY FIRST LIFETIME, I picked up a lot of lies.

Entering the workforce at the tender age of fifteen, I picked up lies.

When I became a mother at the age of seventeen, I picked up lies.

While I was living waist deep in the "single-mom/teacher life," I picked up lies.

As my world flipped upside down becoming an oncology mom, I picked up lies.

My life ended–well my first lifetime–when my 15-year-old son took his last breath in my arms. That's when I picked up the worst lie of all: This is all my fault.

The lies we pick up and hold on to keep us from all that this life has for us. It doesn't matter how big or how small it is, a lie is a lie. If not released back to the pit of hell where it came from, your life can end before it is lived.

PART ONE

MY FIRST LIFETIME

You saw me before I was born. Every day of my life was recorded in Your book. Every moment was laid out before a single day had passed.

Psalm 139:16 NLT

CHAPTER 1

DID MY LIFE BECOME A REALITY SHOW?

Don't remember the sins I committed when I was young.
Don't remember how often I refused to obey You. Remember
me because You love me. Lord, You are good.

Psalm 27:7 NIV

● ● ● ● ● ● ● ● ● ● ●● ● ● ● ●

"I AM KEEPING the baby!" I said with zero hesitation, sitting across from my mother at our dining room table. We had just finished dinner and my mom was always the last one to get up from the table. On most nights, she would sit and read the daily newspaper after dinner, as well as thumb through the mail. Not tonight.

I had waited patiently for everyone else to leave. I knew I needed to rip off the bandage and just come out with it. Eventually people were going to notice the change.

"Well, just let me figure out how to tell your father, he is going to have to know for insurance purposes. How far along do you think you are?"

"Six weeks," I said, not having taken a pregnancy test or knowing which of the days I'd had sex had made me pregnant. My mom's wheels were turning. I could tell I had just thrown her a grenade, and she was holding the pin in place.

No parent wants to hear the words I'm pregnant from their teenage daughter, still a senior in high school. Heck, I don't think a teenager wants to tell her parents those two words ... three if you want to drag it out. What was done was done, and in my 17-year-old brain, there was nothing to look forward to.

The first thing I learned about motherhood was a lie: *Having a baby is the end of my life.*

My family, teachers, church leaders, and friends didn't really know how to be supportive. I mean, I didn't even know I needed support. As my belly slowly grew round and plump, I quickly began to realize what I had gotten myself into.

Making pregnancy announcements wasn't really a thing in high school. I was not the first girl in my grade to get pregnant; there were a handful of us. Using my sonogram picture as my library book's bookmark caused people to ask, "Who's having a baby?"

And for the first time, in front of twenty-five people, I muttered, "It's mine..."

My teacher walked by and repeated what I had said just to make sure she heard me right. Based on her huffing and the rolling of her eyes, she didn't approve.

As soon as news got to the administration that I was pregnant, I was put into a parenting class. I don't really remember learning much in that class. I thought for sure they were going to give me one of those fake baby dolls, you know, the ones that cry, eat, and use the restroom. But no, I never had the pleasure of doing that "as seen on TV" parenting lesson.

My boyfriend, now the father of my child, did not go to my school. He was two years older than me and never could quite control himself enough to stay at one high school long enough to earn any credits. He was the charming bad-boy whose smile made me weak in the knees. We met the summer of my senior year through some mutual friends. He was funny and definitely the life of the party. I did with him what I had done with my few previous boyfriends: I saw him, I wanted him, and I got him. Within a few weeks, we were "together." Within a few months, I was pregnant.

He would drop me off at school and take my car to do God only knows what. I knew I had to finish school and keep working as many hours as I could at a burger place as a carhop. I was determined to be the best mom I could be and not be a statistic.

I really didn't know the odds I was up against.

"Purity culture" is the church culture I grew up in. I was raised in church; we went every Sunday to the early service, every Wednesday, weekend camps, summer camps, walks, retreats, my mom made sure we were all involved to some degree. By "we" I am referring to me, my brothers, and my sister. My dad only went to church on holidays and when we were doing something of importance. I wonder now how my life would have been different if I'd had my dad praying over me every day. I wonder how life would have been different if my family read the Bible together.

I learned what I could in church, especially youth group—reading Bible stories, praying, and learning not to sin. Whatever you do, make sure it isn't sinning. Sins were things like lying, stealing, murdering, and having sex before marriage.

As an eighth grader I made the vow to not have sex before marriage. I knew I could do it. How hard could it be? I told myself, *I need to be a good girl and not sin. God and my parents expect this of me, and I will not have sex before marriage.*

By eighth grade, I also had an interest in boys. Did I have a whole lot of time? No. As a girl who was starting to ride horses competitively, I was either out at the barn or church. There was not a lot of extra time.

That's okay because as an eighth grader, you don't need time to date. All you have to do is have a guy friend that you start to crush on or have class with a boy you think is funny or ride the bus with a boy from around your neighborhood. This was dating in eighth grade as I knew it.

My first boyfriend rode the bus with me. He lived in a different neighborhood less than two miles down the street, but I never saw him outside of school, mostly on the bus. I did have a cell phone at this point in my life. I'd just gotten my first one, actually. We would talk on the phone but not text because texts were ten cents each, sent and received.

He asked me to be his girlfriend, and I said yes.

Then my reputation turned for the worse when I was asked to do things I had never heard of before. My innocence was stripped that day, and I was labeled a prude.

A prude is defined as a person who is or claims to be easily shocked by matters relating to sex or nudity. My eighth grade brain understood this to mean that I was inexperienced and scared, which I was. I knew nothing about sex. It was never talked about in my household. I only heard about it in church (Don't do it until you're married) and in health class (If you are going to do it, wear a condom). My determination to not be who everyone said I was drove me and piqued my curiosity. It was the beginning of my vow being thrown out the window.

My first relationship caused me to believe a lie: *Something is wrong with me.*

By the time I had gotten into high school, the majority (or at least what I felt like was almost everyone) had lost their virginity. More of my innocence began to slip away as I tried my hardest to keep up the culture I had been sheltered from. I began to question everything I was being taught in church and realized my parents had not taught me what I needed to know to survive.

Growing up I can remember us moving from house to house, and my mom traveling for work often. Before the age of five, I had lived in three different states, in four different houses. About halfway through my kindergarten year of school, we moved to Texas and stayed. My older brother and I were kept pretty busy between school and all our extra curricular activities. Ballet, tap, and jazz are where I started my career as a dancer. My music career started with the piano. And my love for horses grew fast after a summer out at the barn.

The time I did have off would be spent looking for what I thought was a missing piece in my life—a best friend. All the girls in school had a best friend, and my older brother had plenty of best friends, too. I spent a lot of time playing with my little brother, but he wasn't best friend material; he was too messy. My barn friends and church friends were just that, barn friends and church friends—very rarely did we hang out outside of those settings. A few of my neighbors were around my age, and we would play, but I always felt like a last resort friend. They'd act like, "We'll play with Ashley if no one else wants to play."

I quickly started to believe another lie: *I don't belong.*

My dad had always carried me around like a prize trophy as a young girl. I knew he loved me and would do anything for me. He was the one who stayed home with me when I was sick or took me to his office. He was my chauffeur, our family's chef, and the house cleaner. A former military man, he ran a tight ship.

We did Indian Princesses, a father-daughter program, for several years. We were in the Tomahawk Tribe with the names Rising Star and Grumpy Bear. I'll let you draw the conclusion of who was who. The one thing my dad didn't do for me was affirm me. I rarely heard the words "I love you" or "You're beautiful." A girl longs to hear these words from her father, and when she doesn't, she accepts it from just any ol' guy.

My mom's desire for her children was for us to be well-rounded, hoping for a bright future for us all. She has always been driven and ambitious. Her corporate career was both a blessing and a curse. I had an amazing childhood with adventure, safety, and joy. But something was missing. It wasn't until my little sister came along that I noticed what was missing. I felt competition enter into my life for the first time, and I was losing.

Do you want to know the nickname my family gave me?

"The oops baby."

My mom got pregnant rather quickly after she had my brother, and—oops!—there was me. It was a funny story to tell, and it made everyone laugh, but as I got older, I started to feel the weight of those words.

Love from my parents was important to me. Love from my siblings and friends was important to me. I wanted not only to be loved, but to *feel* I was loved, to *hear* I was loved.

That deeply personal history motivated me to be a different kind of parent. My baby—my son—was going to know he was wanted and loved beyond the shadow of a doubt. Even if I had to do it all by myself, I was going to be the best mom I could be!

As the days went by, I felt like a whale walking the halls of school and across the graduation stage. I was forced to wear heels, even though I was eight months pregnant.

My relationship with Jayden's father was a roller coaster, causing me an alarming amount of insecurity and doubt. My heart was broken from the beginning of our relationship ... only to get worse as time went on.

The next lie engulfed me like a tidal wave: *I am unworthy.*

I continued riding horses for almost five months into my pregnancy. No one knew I was going to have a baby. Eventually, I started having pain when I sat down. Did you know when you're pregnant your pelvic floor and tailbone soften to prepare your body for birth? Well at the age of 17, I did not.

I ended up bruising my tailbone pretty badly as I was riding one day, and I lied to everyone at the barn, telling them I had fallen while skating as a carhop at work, bruising my tailbone. But a pregnancy is not something you can lie about for long, it starts to show. I knew I couldn't face any more people or their judgments. I was dealing with it every day. One night, around 2 a.m., I drove out to the barn and got all my stuff, without a word or hint to anyone. I feel terrible about this now, but then it seemed like the only way out.

Then, I no longer attended youth nights or rode horses. I went to church with my pregnant belly, heard the comments, saw the looks, felt the judgments, and I no longer felt welcomed.

I would spend the next several months hiding from anyone I knew who would come by the burger place, which was really popular. As time went on, hiding became increasingly harder. Everyone knew by the time nine months rolled around.

On July 17, 2008 around four o'clock in the morning, I woke up with an urgent feeling that I needed to sign up for my first college classes. I waddled my way into the bathroom, then to my laptop. Navigating to the website, I registered for four classes, the minimum requirement for a full-time student. Feeling relieved because I made the deadline for class registration, I closed my laptop and laid back down. On my way down, I felt a pain like I had never felt before.

I ended up in labor and delivery by 9 a.m., getting an epidural a couple hours later, having some complications, and then successfully delivering my baby boy at 5:52 p.m.

I do not know what my birthing expectations had been, but what happened was not it. The epidural really does make you high and loopy. Pushing is exhausting—I almost passed out each time. The first forty-eight hours were painful.

Jayden's dad and I spent three days in the hospital and then off to my parents house we went. By "we" I mean me and my son. His dad was not allowed to stay the night or come over whenever he wanted. My parents wanted to enforce strict rules, making it very clear that they were in charge. This only pushed me out of the house quicker. I was counting down the days until I turned 18 so I could live with my own little family and raise my baby how I wanted to.

CHAPTER 2

COLLEGE WITH A KINDERGARTENER

*I have come to call not those who think they are righteous,
but those who know they are sinners and need to repent.*

Luke 5:32 NLT

● ● ● ● ● ● ● ● ● ● ● ● ● ● ●

"IT'S MOVING DAY!" I reminded my family as I began moving boxes out of my bedroom and on to the driveway to be loaded up in the moving truck.

The excitement was beaming across my face. I imagined this was what typical 18-year-old girls going off to college felt like—a sense of freedom. I did have freedom but not like most girls my age. I had responsibilities and bills added to my plate.

Buying furniture and filling up the fridge with all my favorite foods was thrilling. Having my own schedule and routine, not having to answer to my parents made me feel mature and capable. Everything was a dream at first, but as time went on, I realized I was not only the mother of an infant boy, I was also taking care of his grown dad, too. The weight of life was heavy on my shoulders.

After the domestic violence started I had to find a way out.

I started to plan my escape by solving the main problem: I couldn't afford daycare. Sucking up my pride, I applied for daycare assistance. I was a full-time student and working a full-time job to support my son, making me the picture-perfect candidate for the program. Thankfully, I was accepted. Jayden was enrolled in daycare, and I no longer needed his dad's help to watch him. I asked him to leave, and he did. But the abuse didn't stop.

My only option now was to file a protective order and move back home with my parents. I felt unsafe alone in my apartment and needed help with Jayden on the weekends. I would be lying if I said I didn't feel like a failure; I did. I kept asking myself, *How did I let all this happen? Maybe I'm not as good of a mom as I thought I was.*

I could tell my mom was happy to have us back home, and my dad was glad I was no longer a punching bag. I've only seen my dad cry twice—once when I got pregnant and the other when I told him I was being abused. I was hurt seeing him hurt. It was nice to be home where I felt safe and had a support system, but I knew it was only temporary. With the help of my parents, I was able to take as many classes as I could each semester to finish school so I could start teaching and move out again. I liked being independent.

During those few years at home, I turned 21. I found myself going out after work each night and blowing the money I needed to be saving. I found myself trying to date for the purpose of fun, rather than for marriage building a future. I found myself trying to live the typical young adult college life but I wasn't a typical young adult college girl.

There I was again, trying to figure out where I belonged. I didn't fit in with people my age or with the moms who had kids Jayden's age. Life was hard to navigate because it wasn't just me. Every choice

I made affected Jayden's life, too. There was a lot up against me. I was young and ignorant to the things of motherhood. I was single raising a boy on my own trying to get to a place where we could live life comfortably. As he continued to grow into a young boy, I worried about him and his future.

Jayden was in kindergarten by then. I had looked into the best school options for him, trying to find something that would best fit his very normal, very boyish needs. I knew my son was a handful. Daycare hadn't been a breeze, but his teachers loved him. I also knew he was smart—wise beyond his years. Finally, I found a new charter school. They added Jayden to the waitlist, and I received a call during the summer letting me know that he had been accepted through the lottery. This was exciting news and worked well with my own school and work schedule.

But it wasn't long before I started to get emails and phone calls from the school.

"Jayden won't sit still and do his work"

"Jayden still hasn't finished any of his work for today"

"Jayden hit another student on the playground today"

"Jayden was talking nonstop today"

"Jayden kicked another student on the soccer field"

Jayden, this. Jayden, that.

Meanwhile, I was starting to feel the pressure of my own school responsibilities.

One day, I was working hard at a middle school when I received another call from Jayden's school. I could tell by the tone that this was not good.

"We need you to come pick up Jayden right now. Jayden has gotten into another fight. Right now, he is suspended, and we will be talking about expulsion soon." My heart began to race as I had stepped out into the hallway of my mentor teacher's classroom. It was 10 a.m., and I was doing my student teaching—the most important semester of my college career. I took a deep breath and walked back into the classroom. My emotions were clearly written all over my face.

"Everything okay?" My mentor teacher asked me as her face scrunched up a little, her head tilting slightly to the side. All the students in my class were working on a group project assigned by the teacher.

"Umm ... not really. Jayden has gotten into another fight at school, and they need me to come pick him up." I was embarrassed, trying to be honest without seeming like a terrible mother. My mentor teachers knew about Jayden and the issues we were having in school.

"Go! Go get him! Take the day off. We all have things pop up with our kids. Go!"

"Are you sure?" I didn't know how this was going to reflect on my academic performance, and I had to double check.

"Yes! If you have to go get him, you have to go get him. Go!" She said this very matter-of-factly, like there was no other option. There really wasn't. He was my son, my responsibility, I had to go get him and try to figure something out. This could not keep going on the way it had been. My mind was a flurry of questions.

I arrived at the school to pick up Jayden, and he was sitting in the office by himself with a book. When our eyes met, mine were filled with disappointment and anger while his were filled with shame and apology. If there was one thing about my son that I knew to be true in any circumstance, he never wanted to or intended to disappoint me or upset me to any degree.

I listened to what the principal had to say. To me it sounded like no adults saw this happen, and they were going off of the testimonies of five-year-old kids.

It became clear to me that my son was a target, and I had to get him out of this heartless school environment. The next day, I withdrew him from the charter school and enrolled him into a private, half-day kindergarten program. Finally, he began thriving! He was reading by the second week, learning more in a half day than he had in a full day at the other school. He didn't get in trouble for breathing or talking. And most of all, his teacher loved him.

It's interesting what the feeling of love can do for us from a very young age.

CHAPTER 3

I AM NOT A
STATISTIC

I can do all things through Christ who strengthens me.

Philippians 4:13 NKJV

• • • • • • • • • • •• • • • •

THE TASSEL OF my graduation cap dangled in front of my face, as I recorded a social media video to send out to all my peeps. The day had finally come for me to graduate college, after six years of hard work. It took me six years, but I did it! You know that whole four-year degree thing? Well, that wasn't a realistic timeframe for a single, working mom.

My family all came to celebrate my big day. The ceremony was long and boring with no viral-worthy moments. I walked the stage, took pictures, and that was that. I was a commuter and didn't bond in college the way most people my age did. I didn't sleep in the dorms or play on a team; the experience was different for me. Nevertheless, college was over, and I had now entered into another realm of adulthood: finding a career.

I graduated in the spring of 2014, and by August, I still didn't have a job. I had just moved out of my parents' house into a beautiful, luxury apartment with only the credit card I had just been approved for as spending money. My mom and sister were going on a little road trip and wanted to take Jayden. I would later meet them when they made it to Galveston for some seafood and beach time.

"Have you heard anything about a job yet, sweetie?" my mom asked me as we were walking around the boardwalk.

"No, I've applied everywhere I can think of. Worst case scenario I'll just be a substitute teacher to get my foot in the door at a district." I gave a big sigh, but my statement came out very straightforward, like that was a final decision. I had always known I wanted to be a teacher. From a very young age, my first grade teacher would let me take her extra copies of assignments home to give to my "class," which consisted of some stuffed animals and imaginary people. Teaching was the only thing on my radar.

"What about Jayden, where will he be going for first grade?" Now I felt like I was being grilled, as if I were being irresponsible.

"I don't know, I guess our zoned school." I still hadn't registered him yet. The whirlwind of thoughts in my head started again: *Maybe I am being irresponsible. Maybe I did move out of my parents' house too quickly again. Maybe this is all a really bad idea. No, I can do this. Come on Lord.*

That evening, I received a phone call for a phone interview the following Monday. I did the interview as we were driving back home, and the call dropped multiple times. The interview was for a fifth-grade math teacher position at an elementary school. With all my student teaching and training received in a middle school, I had a keen interest in a middle school position. But this elementary school principal assured me that I would only be teaching math and would have just three classes a day, instead of six. She sold me on the idea of an elementary school, offered me the job, and I accepted.

There, now I had a career. I am so not a statistic.

The way the job worked out at the last minute and the fact that it was an elementary school so Jayden was able to enroll and go to school with me was perfect. It was an answered prayer I didn't even know I was praying. God knew where He wanted us to be.

With only one week left before my first official day of work, I frantically ran around from store to store picking out the needs and decor for my very first classroom. Elementary teachers put a whole lot more effort into the aesthetic part of their classroom than middle-school teachers did. I made the effort and still fell short, but as soon as 25 fifth-grade bodies (and all their belongings) came in the door, the room instantly felt cluttered with all kinds of personalities.

Just because Jayden was in the same building didn't mean his behavior magically disappeared. I was having deja vu, seeing notes in his planner every day and getting emails at the end of each week. I started feeling frustrated.

I couldn't figure it out. Jayden was good at home and listened well. Was he busy? Yes. Did he ask a lot of questions? Yes. Did he like to roughhouse? Yes, but he was six years old and needed patience while he learned. I met with his teacher and helped her strategize, I held Jayden accountable and often got others involved. I was desperate to help my son succeed in school and in life.

I shared my concerns with my best friend Stefanie, whom I've known since church camp in the second grade, but we didn't exactly know it until we reunited again in middle school. She told me about a church she was now attending that her husband grew up in. She had nothing but good things to say and thought it may be a good thing for Jayden. After all, she was his godmother.

It didn't take long to decide we should give it a try. The kid's ministry was hosting Stronger Nights during the Wednesday night service. I dropped off Jayden in a room full of smiling faces and warm welcomes. There was an indoor playground with a basketball area so I knew Jayden would be just fine.

Then I walked across the parking lot to the church's main building just in awe of what I was seeing and experiencing. First of all, this place was huge, not like the church I had grown up in. Second, there was diversity like I had never seen in one room. I walked down the center aisle to sit in one of the cushioned, stadium-style seats and took a deep breath. Worship was about to start as the instruments rolled to welcome all who were in the room.

It was amazing! I saw clapping. I saw dancing. I saw hands lifted. I saw people crying. I saw heads bowed, and eyes closed. This was not the hymnal worship experience I was used to. I continued to look around while I sang, leaving my hands gently touching the back of the seat in front of me so they would have something to do. I didn't know how or when to put them in the air. The expression of worship coming from the people of this house was something I longed for.

After that service I felt different and very curious about the new feeling. I went to pick up Jayden, and he was smiling from ear to ear. He seemed to have had the same experience as me because he wouldn't stop telling me all about it.

"How was the big church for you, mommy?" He finally asked me after he had shared his own worship experience of lifting his hands. My son had always been full of courage and bravery, never afraid to express his love to Jesus.

"Big church was awesome, baby! Mommy would like to come back on Sunday. Would you?" My eyes peered in the rearview mirror to see his face instantly light up. This was very different from all the conversations we'd had on our way home from school each day. There was joy and excitement in my son's eyes rather than shame and apology. I was determined that I would continue to find things for him where I saw this same joy.

The following day I called the church to see if they had a mentor program for boys. They did not, but they assured me the male leaders they had were strong and would pour into my son.

When Sunday came, I dropped off Jayden and went to service. I continued to feel amazed and at home the whole time. Then I went to pick up Jayden and just so happened to see the kids' pastor. I asked him about my need for a mentor, and it was obvious that my earlier phone call had already been passed on. He talked to me for a few minutes and assured me they would help in any way that they could.

I could never have predicted how perfectly God had arranged the timing of our joining that church. Godly male mentorship and support was about to become unbelievably important in Jayden's life.

Just a few months later, I woke up to an alarming amount of text messages, social media messages, and missed calls. Jayden's dad was dead. He had been murdered.

It was barely six-thirty in the morning, and I picked up the phone to call Stefanie. By the way she answered, I knew she already knew why I was calling.

"Did I make a mistake, Stefanie? Did I scar Jayden for life? This was not how it was supposed to go!" I began to sob.

I was starting to hear another lie: *I am to blame for Jayden not knowing his dad.*

"Ashley, none of this is your fault." She reassured me that I could have never seen this coming nor do anything to change what had happened.

Up until then, he would ask about his dad from time to time, but I never knew his whereabouts. I had no idea how I was going to tell Jayden that his father was gone forever. It was so important to me to handle the situation well that I made the school counselor aware of what was going on and asked for her advice on how to break it to Jayden. I mean is there really a correct way to tell a child their dad is dead? I did the best I knew how.

"Jayden?" I said softly while peering through the rearview mirror.

His big, beautiful brown eyes looked up towards me.

"You know how you've been asking mommy where your dad is?"

He nodded with a curious look in his eyes.

"Well, I found out that he is in heaven."

Immediately, his bottom lip quivered, and the curiosity turned to tears rolling down his face. I reach my hand back behind me to rub his leg to comfort him. Looking back, I wish I had waited until I was sitting with him so I could have hugged him.

He cried for a while, and when I laid him down for bed, he wanted to talk. Sharing with him what happened in language appropriate for a six-year-old child, I was able to calm some of the heightened anxiety of the unknown. I had determined in my mind that taking him to the funeral would be the best thing for him in the long run so I looked into the obituaries to find the funeral information.

When we arrived, we sat in the back. Jayden looked around to see his face everywhere, on the pamphlet, on people's shirts, in pictures all around.

"Does everyone know me here?" he asked me with a worried look on his face. I wasn't sure and told him we would talk about it in the car because the service was already taking place. After the service, viewing the body, and meeting with family afterwards I left the funeral feeling defeated, and Jayden felt confused.

Something started to change in me over the next couple of years. I cared less and less about going out and dating, and more and more about my son and my career. Being a mom became my pride and joy. Jayden was the greatest accomplishment in my life. He was doing well in school, involved in church, and playing a variety of sports.

That old lie that motherhood would ruin my life started to crumble, and I learned the truth: *Motherhood is the greatest gift God has given me.*

Everything started to change. I started seeking and searching for God like I had never done before. I was attending my new church on a regular basis, involved in a small group, and taking some of the classes they were offering. I was hungry for the Lord! I started praying daily and journaling, occasionally reading my Bible and learning how to study it. Sometimes, Jayden and I would do these things together. Philippians 4:13 started to come alive, I really could do all things through Christ who strengthens me.

Jayden's Prayer
10/23/2016
My Lord Almighty, when we fall, lift us up. Our life be a journey and the Lord be faithful in Jesus name we pray, Amen!

CHAPTER 4

WHEN WE WERE BOTH IN 5TH GRADE

This is My command—be strong and courageous!
Do not be afraid or discouraged. For the Lord your God
is with you wherever you go.
Joshua 1:9 NLT

● ● ● ● ● ● ● ● ● ● ● ● ● ● ● ●

"MOM! ARE YOU going to be my teacher?" Jayden asked. He was finally in the 5th grade with me, and boy, was he ready. By that time, I had made quite the name for myself on campus. Everyone knew Ms. Selby was loud and loved math. Everyone knew Ms. Selby doesn't play around, but then again, is always playing around. Everyone knew Ms. Selby was Jayden Simmons' mom.

He was almost a student on my roster, but our school was growing, and we added a fourth section to our fifth-grade team the year before. That meant I had to teach another subject, which was science. It was not my favorite thing in the world. I honestly felt like I was learning with the kids at times. I mean, who remembers what they learned in fifth-grade science? What I discovered as a teacher is that you can take as many classes and trainings as you want, but the real learning doesn't happen until you have students in front of you, testing your every word. The kids could easily tell math was my jam and that science was the sticky peanut butter that made it hard to talk.

The new school year started off smoothly. I had declared that this would be my most spiritual year, yet. I vowed to study my Bible more, pray more, journal more, and even read more books! I had always disliked reading. Personally, I think most of that came from my time in elementary school. I was the student who always read ahead when doing "popcorn reading" to make sure I knew how to read every word on that page before it was my turn. I wasn't the best writer either. I failed state tests and had to have special tutoring in school. My parents even paid for outside tutoring services.

I struggled in school, but I knew I *wanted* to enjoy reading. At 27 years old, I set a goal of reading one book each month and ended up reading 25 books that year. It was a big turn around year for me. I was doing things I hadn't really done before. I was setting goals that were outside of my comfort zone and achieving them. I was falling in love with this growth trajectory I was on.

I was tired of trying to find love in this world. Dating had not been easy or successful for me. I wanted to fall in love with myself and learn the love of my Heavenly Father in a way I had never known before. The enemy knew I wanted this, and just like he did with Eve, he would tempt me. He would use my past against me and have me questioning my identity as a daughter of the Most High. But I kept reminding myself that wasn't me any more, I would not be so easily shaken!

Jayden was on his own path of success. He was maturing and becoming quite the athlete. He played football in the fall and basketball in the spring. I could only handle one sport per season. Little League is no joke. Two to three practices a week plus a game on the weekends.

Jayden was making good grades and making a name for himself at church by always showing up. He loved serving. I loved watching him do it and was proud to have him alongside me at school. He was beginning to learn the weight of each choice he had to make and counting the cost, being open with me about his struggles. We were becoming quite the little pair, indestructible. My journal reflected renewed hope.

Ashley's Journal

9/3/2018

I cannot believe it is September! 2018 is flying by. I have really tried to focus this year on You Lord, and making this my most spiritual year of my life to this point. I've done a lot of things this year, thanks be to God. I rededicated myself back to You God, I served Your city, I became a member, I started serving on a Dream Team, I have read more than ever before, I have spent more time with You God, and I have been a bridge and a branch for others. As I write it all out and look at where I came from, I know You are with me. For the rest of this year I want to sink into the Bible! I want to hear from You Lord! Amen.

God has done too many good works in my life for me not to believe. I need to let go of control and surrender it to the Lord. He knows much better than I do. I am His sheep—I will listen and follow His voice.

Jesus has been knocking on my heart, and sometimes I open and other times I pretend I'm not home. I need to listen for His knock and always be ready to open with listening ears. I want to let Him in and not run away to fix my own issues. Love into love.

Lord forgive me for pretending not to be home. I will let You in!

Sunday before the New Year, Jayden and I decided to get baptized together. Both of us had already been baptized with the sprinkling of the water on our foreheads, but now we felt compelled to go under the water, and felt the need to do it together.

What a Beautiful Name by Hillsong Worship was being sung as Jayden entered the water. I stood next to the pool, proud to see my son making a public declaration to everyone in the room—he was choosing Jesus. Under the water he went, coming out with a bright smile and shaking the water off him like a dog just given a bath. Tears started to fill my eyes as he exited the pool, and I entered.

"Is that your son?" Our pastor asked me.

"Yes, sir!"

"Great job, mom!"

It was only by the grace of God that we were both here, choosing Him, saying yes to the call. Under the water I went, coming out of it refreshed, excited for what was going to happen next.

On January 1, I prayed for three things:

1. Grow closer to God
2. Grow closer to Jayden
3. My next career move

Little did I know that at the beginning of March I would be blindsided and have all three of those prayers answered.

Blindsided is an understatement.

My parents had given Jayden a basketball camp experience for Christmas. The timing was perfect. The camp was held the first few days of the new year, giving me some quiet time alone to plan out our year. When I went to pick up Jayden the first day, the coach explained to me how Jayden may have sprained his knee. I looked closely. Jayden was walking just fine so I was confused. I thought maybe this was one of the I'm-injured-so-I-can't-help-clean-up type of injuries, but I kept an eye on it. We iced and elevated his knee, and it seemed to be just fine. He finished the basketball camp with no other problems.

Only a month later, we were walking down three flights of stairs from our apartment to our car when his knee just gave out, and he fell. Jayden caught himself on the rails, and he only missed a step or two, but suddenly his knee was hurting and starting to swell again. We iced it, we elevated it. He took a hot bath and put on a brace. His knee got better, but then it got worse. A couple weeks passed in this see-saw pattern. Things were looking better, then they weren't, then they were, then they weren't.

One morning, I peered up from my Bible. The sun hadn't even come up, and Jayden was crawling on the floor, crying in pain, and unable to walk. I picked up all eighty pounds of him and saw his knee was red, inflamed, and warm to the touch. I called my principal immediately because I was going to need the day off. Next, I called an urgent care facility. I needed to know if they had an x-ray machine because my son's leg appeared to be broken.

We got an appointment quickly but ended up waiting a long time. Putting Jayden in a wheelchair, they took him back to the x-ray room.

Minutes later he was back with me, and before we could gather our thoughts, the doctor was in our room with a referral to an oncologist.

"I don't know what it is, but it appears your son has a tumor in his bone." He pointed to the x-ray image and the discoloration.

Stunned, I just said, "Okay."

We left with no answers, a lot of confusion, and if I'm being honest, some fear. My mind spun with questions.

I called my family and close friends to ask for prayer. Every time I mentioned "tumor" they would cry. Interestingly, I wasn't crying. I wasn't going to worry until I knew for sure.

We got an appointment for the next morning.

To this day, I can walk into the hospital and think of that day. The smell of the lobby is very distinct. I've been there two other times since this day and both times the smell gave me pause. Going up the elevator, we both held our breath and prayed our own little, silent prayers.

As we approached the oncology office, I opened the waiting room door and noticed we were both the youngest ones there.

"Simmons!" they called out.

We smiled nervously at everyone who made eye contact as we made our way through the hall to the exam room.

We told the nurse what was going on, and then told the doctor.

The oncologist mentioned that he had looked at the x-rays, and as he was about to continue he paused and motioned for me to come outside of the room. He led me over to a computer to show me the same discoloration the other doctor had shown me. On a piece of paper he wrote: Osteosarcoma and Ewing Sarcoma. Holding his pen between his fingers he pointed to osteosarcoma.

"I'm pretty sure this is the one, but we won't know without a biopsy. I am referring you to Dallas."

Still confused, I gave the doctor permission to tell Jayden. I had no idea what was happening or about to happen. I could not comprehend that my son had cancer. I was sure I was being punished. This had to be my fault.

A new lie settled in my mind and made itself at home: *I have done this to my son.*

Nothing can fully prepare you for life-changing news. Even more, nothing can fully prepare you for the way a child responds to life-changing news.

"Am I going to die?" Jayden said as we were driving back home. I could understand the question—all he knew about cancer was that it happened to old people, usually right before they died.

"No, you're not going to die." I responded as if what he was saying was absolutely ridiculous.

Actually, I was asking myself the same questions: *Could he die? How bad is this? Did we catch it early? We could pray for a miracle! How do I pray for this? God, I need You.*

It was from that moment on, I started to take God even more seriously.

By the grace of God, that day was a Wednesday and church was in session. Jayden cried as people asked him why he had a brace and crutches. The words couldn't quite come out of either of our mouths.

"We found out today that he has a tumor in his leg," was all I could manage to get out. I dropped him off with the other kids, and I walked to big church. I ended up falling to my knees at the altar by the end of service. I was crying out to the Lord, not with words, just my tears. I had no idea what to pray for.

I would later find out that the kids ministry had had a special service for Jayden. They allowed his godfather to stay with him, which gave him great comfort. I was grateful as well because I needed some time with God. The kids' pastor called Jayden on stage, asking all the children to stretch their hands towards him and pray for healing.

It was the perfect night to the worst day.

Jayden ended up sleeping with me "just in case he didn't wake up."

And my heart broke.

CHAPTER 5

THE FIRST 90 DAYS AFTER DIAGNOSIS

*See, God has come to save me. I will trust in Him
and not be afraid. The Lord God is my strength
and my song; He has given me victory.*

Isaiah 12:2 NLT

● ● ● ● ● ● ● ● ● ● ● ● ● ● ●

"CAN I PLEASE see your insurance card and ID?" the receptionist
said kindly, handing me a stack of paperwork to fill out.

Reaching into my bag for my wallet, I smiled and then went to sit
down next to Jayden with the clipboard in my hand. We both looked
around at this new place we would soon call our second home. There
were puzzles and books galore and a foosball table in a little room
with a giant couch, mimicking a children's cartoon setting.

"For Simmons," I heard the receptionist call for us. Perking up, I
made my way over to her. "Ma'am, we don't have a referral from your
PCP. Who is your primary care physician?" This was the first of many
run-ins with insurance and their rules.

I gave her the name of Jayden's pediatrician because she was someone we loved and trusted. They informed me that she was not in network with my insurance provider and that I would need to find a new PCP.

I already knew she wasn't in network because I had been paying out of pocket for all our visits. When ObamaCare happened, the insurance world and rules changed, big time. I didn't feel it necessary to change our pediatrician, who had been Jayden's doctor since the day he was born.

"Whatever the cost of this appointment, I'll pay it out of pocket and then get all this sorted out." My son had cancer, and I was willing to do anything.

During that first appointment, Jayden had his blood drawn and was asked if he or I had any questions. We did not. They set up our first admission for the following week to give us time to figure out insurance.

At the first opportunity, I frantically called Jayden's pediatrician office, and was met with nothing but obstacles.

"There isn't any way for y'all to give a referral?" At this stage in the game I thought a referral was like a recommendation, the same way you refer someone to an apartment complex or auto shop. I had no idea that this was the new process. My son was never significantly ill before this. All his visits were well-visits or ADHD management, with an occasional sick visit. The receptionist on the other end of the phone kindly explained the process to me, and I understood. We were now going to have to find a new doctor, one we trusted to help us.

I then called my insurance broker, who had also become a family friend over the years. He helped me find a new PCP for Jayden. He even reference-checked her for me. We got an appointment within a couple of days. When we arrived for the appointment, there were even more obstacles.

"Ma'am, unfortunately your insurance card doesn't show the doctor as Jayden's PCP, we won't be able to see him today."

"You're kidding!" I said, upset. I wasn't agitated with her but with the system and the fact that policy is more important than my son, agonizing pain and needing help. "What do I need to do? He has to be seen today."

She explained to me what I had to do but seemed very doubtful that I was going to be able to get what I needed. I stepped out into the hall and started making phone calls to my insurance company.

"This is cancer, not a common cold!" I said, raising my voice. "I am not getting off this phone until you get me what I need. What my son needs!" Tears of frustration and sadness welled up and trickled down my face. I had had it! I was not going to be put on hold again or transferred, I was going to get this stupid name on this stupid card, and for crying out loud, they were going to back-date it!

I came back inside to hand the receptionist a reference number to the fact that we did indeed have the information we needed in order to have our appointment. The referral was sent to the oncologist, and we were all set for our first admission on Tuesday.

Ashley's Journal

March 12, 2019

It's been exactly a week since I got the news. I am still living in a dream of if this is really real, but being that I'm on a little blue plastic couch at Medical City Children's Hospital in Dallas, I'd say it's pretty real. My baby is being strong and keeping his spirits up. We are so loved and feel God all over us!

Hospital round number two started today. Check in with Dr. Goldman, and then admission into the hospital for a bone biopsy. The check up went fine and insurance is hopefully all taken care of! The biopsy was quick and easy, but the pain I saw my baby in, as well as the drugged state, scared me. Not seeing him laughing or joking, but in and out of consciousness was scary. I know this is part of the fight, but that doesn't make it any less scary. The worst is yet to come in this war.

I plan on taking this day by day, moment by moment, and not missing any time with my dear sweet baby! I am at peace with the situation right now, until I am given a reason to panic. It is spring break so work is not a worry, I have money in the bank so food and gas are not a worry. My house is taken care of so my environment is not a worry. My car is in a parking garage so my transportation is not a worry. Most importantly, my baby is next to me in great hands, and he is never a worry!

March 15, 2019

Today has been a very rough day! I was up all night worrying and nervous for the next surgery and the beginning of chemo. Our morning started right at 7:45 for a full-body bone scan. We got the results back and learned the cancer is only in his leg! Praise God for that great news!! After that he went to get his port put in. He did very well in surgery, but came out with extremely high blood pressure again. As they gave him pain meds and made him more comfortable his blood pressure went down. He gets so many compliments on how great of a kid he is and as his mom, that makes me feel so good!

We had tons of visitors today! My mom of course, the Thurman's, Steve and Alicia, and Mrs. Simone and her girls. So much love has been shown to us I just can't even thank everyone enough! Jayden also found out he won't be able to attend school anymore. I am hoping and praying that I will be able to be his home-bound teacher! I am qualified and can take care of him best!

Tomorrow morning we start chemo and I am very nervous. The doctors keep telling me all about the side effects. I am standing firm in my faith that God will cancel out major side effects and allow Jayden to go through treatment with minimal pain! Our prayer warriors are on the loose, and we will not stop until FULL healing is over my baby! I am hoping to get a good night's sleep tonight because tomorrow is going to be long. I don't know what to expect, but I ask God for the strength and faith to make it through tomorrow and the 7-10 days following chemo, IN JESUS NAME! AMEN!!

Within ten days of diagnosis my son had two surgeries, four scans, and started chemo. There were no longer feelings of this being a dream. Everything was very real and happening very fast. The doctor asked if we wanted to start chemo right away or wait a day to let the port heal. My mind could not wrap itself around the pace of everything. I looked at Jayden to make sure he agreed with me to start tomorrow. I mean, the kid had just gotten out of surgery and still had tears in his eyes. I couldn't imagine asking him to do another thing that day. More visitors came through, really cheering him up.

When it came to chemo, he was mostly worried about his hair, and the doctors let him know it wouldn't fall out right away but within the next month or so. That made him feel a little better but not really. The lovely nurses started to run his hydration fluids because you have to be at a certain level of hydration before starting chemo. Following his fluids, there were premeds in his IV. These were supposed to help with any nausea he may have. Once the final beep went off to show the premeds were complete, two nurses with full-on hazmat protection walked in with a yellow trash can and a syringe full of red liquid—doxorubicin, known as "the red devil."

Five minutes later, chemo started. Thirty minutes later, vomiting started and didn't stop until more meds were given. I quickly learned how to deal with Jayden vomiting. It was the one bodily function that I couldn't handle. If I hear you throwing up, I'm gagging. If I smell it, I'm throwing up, too. But when your child is helpless and can't catch their breath, you learn to deal with it and be there in the midst of the horror.

Jayden needed to stay at the hospital after his treatment, and within a couple of days, I realized that Jayden was going to be needing me around the clock, and I began to worry about my job, my career, my students, and my teaching team. I asked the nurses their opinion about going through treatment and working. They echoed each other, letting me know that it was going to be hard, considering how this oncology world is very unpredictable. I was currently on FMLA, the Family and Medical Leave Act, and I had been given twelve weeks of unpaid leave to come to a decision.

To our surprise a brand new pediatric oncology wing was opening that week. Jayden was the star of the show, riding in their little mini sports car up and down the hall lined with doctors, nurses, techs, and other hospital staff cheering for the grand opening. We settled in nicely in this brighter, more spacious, family unit. Jayden liked that there was a bigger TV with an HDMI port for games. I slept better on the foldout twin size bed, which was nice and firm, like my bed at home. Things were starting to perk up.

"If Jayden is able to eat a couple meals and hold them down, you might get to go home today," our nurse said one day, trying to encourage Jayden without making promises she wasn't sure she could keep.

Jayden sucked in a quick, excited breath. "Really?" That was all he needed to hear. He snapped his neck, looking toward me, "Mom, give me the menu!"

I slid the menu over to him, he ordered a meal, and we got to go home later that day.

My brother met me at my house. We lived on the third floor, and I was too tired to carry Jayden up the stairs, along with all our stuff from the hospital. I was working on being transferred to a first floor apartment, but it wasn't going to happen for a few months. My brother picked up Jayden ever so gently and walked him up the stairs. The moment they got to the top, Jayden started to throw up everywhere. It was devastating.

The lies were piling up. I kept thinking: *I can't do this. I am inadequate as a caregiver.*

"Okay, let's just get him inside and I'll clean this up," I said, trying to remain calm because I knew Jayden was watching me. He couldn't bear seeing me sad or worried. He wanted everything to go back to normal just as much as I did.

"Lay him down, and I'll get his stuff all set up," I directed my brother. I had been directing him ever since I was born. We were a little over a year apart and God saw it fit for me to be my brother's keeper. After laying Jayden down, he went to finish bringing up all the stuff from my car. It wasn't easy for my brother, seeing his nephew like this. It wasn't easy for Jayden, either. He didn't want anyone to see him like this.

The nausea just wouldn't stop. Before completely freaking out, I called the doctor. They sent in a new medication to add into our rotation.

I resigned from my job. I didn't exactly know where I was going to get money for treatment, bills, rent, and food, but I knew Jayden needed me. He was my top priority.

A big step of faith for me was testing the tithe principle in the Bible. I started tithing in the summer of 2017, believing God to be the provider of my household. Living as a single mom on a teacher's salary, I struggled. Giving 10% before spending a dime was not easy, but I have never looked back or regretted the decision to tithe, ever.

Our new normal consisted of being home for a few days then at the hospital for a week. This went on and on for three months. Jayden endured two full cycles of chemo, which included six rounds of three different chemotherapy drugs—doxorubicin, cisplatin, and methotrexate.

Next up was surgery.

There were three options:

1. An internal prosthetic—which meant multiple more possible surgeries and no sports.

2. A donor bone graft—which meant longer recovery, more possible surgeries, and no sports.

3. An amputation—which meant a prosthetic leg and going back to running, playing sports, and doing all the things he loved.

Playing basketball with his friends and being able to run around the parking lot at church were what mattered to Jayden. He made the decision to get his leg amputated.

He was quieter on the day of surgery. I would ask my usual mom questions and get one-to-two-word answers, hinting to me that he wasn't interested in talking. I respected his boundaries and just let him know I'm always here. I parked the car, took a deep breath, and we walked inside the sliding glass doors for yet another hospital admission. But this time, it felt different.

We knew he wouldn't be leaving the same.

Neither of us expected the trauma that came with amputation. When Jayden came out from under the power of anesthesia, he cried for hours. I had never seen him like this. He was in pain both physically and mentally, unable to see out of the black hole of losing his leg.

The next day he perked up and got out of bed. Jayden wouldn't stay down for long.

He struggled a little at first but quickly got the hang of having just one leg. Physical therapy was painful but so important for the longevity of his partial leg. Eventually, we would call it his "stump," but at first, his partial leg was a very touchy subject.

A few weeks later, he started chemo again, and we were back on the roller coaster of treatment. We would be home for a few days, then at the hospital for a week, home for a few days, then at the hospital for a week.

This continued for five months.

CHAPTER 6

OUR CHRISTMAS MIRACLE

*I remain confident of this: I will see the goodness of the Lord
in the land of the living.*

Psalm 27:13 NIV

● ● ● ● ● ● ● ● ● ● ● ● ● ● ● ●

THE DAY BEFORE Thanksgiving, at 8:30 in the morning, Dr. Goldman called. I knew that couldn't be good. I hated waiting on scan results. In the oncology world, families call it scan-xiety. The days leading up to scans, as well as the days that follow, are full of apprehension of the unknown.

"We got Jayden's final scans back, and there appears to be a little something on his right lung," the doctor said.

My heart sank. "Okay, so what does that mean?" I didn't really know if I wanted the answer to my question.

"Well, we've got to remove it. I'll send these results to the surgical team and have them reach out to you." His voice was so calm and positive.

"Okay, thank you."

"Yeah, not the news we wanted, but we will get him taken care of!" he said confidently.

We ended our conversation, and I got out of bed, making my way to my prayer closet. I fell to my knees and lost it.

"Why is this happening?! Did I not have enough faith? What did I do wrong? Why God? Why? Save my son!"

As my heart was breaking, the lies started to whisper again: *Maybe my faith isn't as strong as I think it is.*

Ashley's Journal
Thanksgiving Day 2019

Imagine being in an escape room. You have one hour to complete the challenge awaiting you. For the next hour your heart is racing, you're running around like crazy, looking at everything around you and why is it there? Do we need this? What is this? Oh look numbers, yes! Next clue. Sixty minutes of trying to figure out a puzzle not everyone has been able to accomplish. You're rocking it, ten minutes left and you have the last clue figured out. Hoping this is the clue to unlock the door to escape. Boom. The door opens and there is a whole other room to figure out. Time to figure out the last clues in the last room before you can escape. Today I felt like I just opened that escape room door number two.

I woke up this morning to the words cancer *written over my head again. I hadn't felt this way since March, when all this started. And again in June when the leg was gone. Now in November it begins again—what seems to be a neverending battle. And*

Thanksgiving week, at that. Like I'm supposed to be thankful for this. How can I be thankful for this? What is going to come out of this? Why us again? We did everything the doctors said and followed the treatment plan. What happened?

Osteosarcoma, pediatric osteosarcoma, at that! My son now has spots on his lungs. The doctor felt concerned enough to call me the day before Thanksgiving to tell me Jayden will need a biopsy. This time the biopsy will be in the lung, umm scary! The internet isn't helping either, but I can't help but to look and see what they say. What can I be thankful for today?

I don't want to slum around and cry all day, so the question needs to be answered: What can I be thankful for today? Well, I can be thankful for typing this. Being alive and breathing, getting ready to cook green beans and cornbread casserole. Worship music. Listening to encouraging and uplifting music is perfect right now. My son, sleeping peacefully in his room. The rain outside, making little water droplet noises. My home. I live in a great place surrounded by good people. My family. Spending time with my mom and dad, my grandma, Gracie, and Haley! I'm going to miss Ryan and Sam this year. Big time. My car. It's still going! I prayed for that! Our prayer warriors. Any news I have and put out there for people to see, a swarm of warriors, an army of heaven, surrounds us, builds us up, and lifts us up in prayer. I know God can hear all of us down here! Right here. I can be thankful for that. Thank you Lord. I can be thankful.

Being thankful is one thing, but my prayer is of another. I need healing for my son. Jayden Xavier Simmons, born July 17, 2008, at 5:52pm, needs healing. It is all in your hands God. I am scared and worried, but I'm thankful. Thank You for all You have blessed me with. Keep Jayden close. Make him a priority, please. Cover him with the blood of Jesus, Your one and only Son. Get rid of any cancer in his body! May he live a long full life. You are a good Father. In Your precious name I pray. Amen.

Surgery was scheduled for December 17, 2019. Jayden was going to have a thoracotomy. When we met with the surgeon he explained how he would make an incision between Jayden's ribs. He would then take his lung out between two of the ribs and feel all over it. If there were any tumors he would be able to feel the rice-like clump of cells. Essentially these tumors were like pieces of bone in Jayden's lung. He would then put everything back, pushing the lung back in place, sliding it between the two ribs, closing him up with sutures inside and outside of the incision, and placing a chest tube for drainage.

We were in this same weird space and time where things were explained but expectations were ambiguous. The usual checklist of documents was required. I had to fill out his medical history yet again, sign consent, and watch them mark the correct area and side. Jayden was given some "silly juice" and felt just fine. I, on the other hand, was a nervous wreck! They rolled him back to the operating room, and I walked to the waiting room taking a deep breath as I sat down.

Gazing around the room I took inventory. There was a family of four with blankets spread out, along with some snacks. There was also a young couple, hand in hand, watching the news on a TV that was too loud. There was the live surgery board that had patients' initials and status listed. People came and went for the next couple of hours. My airpods stayed in my ears, worship music calming me and bringing me back to a place of peace. I read a devotional book, with my Bible open and ready for a Word from the Lord.

Two hours later, I was the only one in the waiting room. I looked up and saw his surgical nurse approaching me.

"Jayden's mom?"

I nodded.

"Don't worry, everything is okay!" She must have seen the worry written all over my face. "Sorry it is taking longer than we expected. The doctor has called down radiology and the ultrasound team. He hasn't been able to find anything." She kept talking, but I could no longer listen. It was a miracle. I had always read stories about things like this but had never experienced it myself, and I was in shock.

"It should only be another hour or so, and the doctor will come chat with you." I smiled and nodded again, staying silent.

Without hesitation, I began to type up my praise report to send out to all our prayer warriors. I wouldn't dare send it until I spoke with the doctor, but my soul was feeling the glory of God in the air. Sure enough, about an hour later the doctor came out with his hands in the air, shoulders shrugging. "I don't know what to tell you. It was clear on the scan but I felt nothing. I called radiology down, and they tagged the spot, still nothing."

"Sounds like a Christmas miracle to me!" There was no hiding my excitement.

"They will come get you when he is a little more awake." He took a deep breath. "I'll come by tomorrow to see how he is doing."

"Thank you!"

I sent my praise report out to the masses. Everyone was about to know what just happened to my son. What my eyes had witnessed! What my ears had heard! The doctor couldn't find anything. Thirty minutes went by, and I was becoming restless, ready to be with my son and kiss his forehead. He was my little miracle.

But my joy and excitement would soon dwindle when I saw him. Still very much out of it from all the meds, he had tears in the corners of his eyes. He was breathing short, shallow breaths.

I bent over to whisper in his ear. "I'm here, Jayden. Mommy is here."

As I rubbed his hand, he opened his eyes slightly, and all I could see was pure pain—pain that didn't allow him to speak with words. It would be an hour or so before Jayden was stable enough to head upstairs to our hospital room for the next few days.

The healing process consisted of draining all the excess fluid through Jayden's chest tube. As you can imagine, after his lung was taken out of the body and handled for hours, it was pretty inflamed. He had to drain less than 50cc in a twenty-four hour period before they could take the tube out. He was draining well over 200cc a day.

That year, we had spent Mother's Day, Easter, and both our birthdays in the hospital. Christmas was quickly approaching, and I was praying for the Lord to give us the gift of a holiday at home.

We ended up on the news that week, telling our miracle story. We were the talk of the whole oncology floor.

A newly diagnosed family arrived during that time. Taking it upon ourselves to welcome and encourage them, Jayden gave the little girl some great advice, "Trust the nurses and doctors."

We were quickly becoming the oncology floor's liaison team! I joked that I was like the mayor of 6NW! And God was doing His thing—the thing He was doing the entire time. Bringing people to us, bringing us to people, sharing our story, sharing our faith, and accelerating Jayden's healing so we could have one more Christmas miracle: home.

Ashley's Journal

Christmas Eve 2019

It's Christmas Eve and 4:39 a.m. We just got home from a seven day, six night stay at the hospital, you'd think I'd be sleeping so good, but no. Here I am up. Almost wide awake. I don't know if it's because I'm worried about my beloved son in the other room, who has been sleeping since 7:00 p.m., or if I'm just overwhelmed with emotions that I don't know how to express, or if I'm just used to not sleeping good at this point in time? Who knows!

I am thankful to be home for Christmas. Thankful for all my blessings. Thankful for our Christmas miracle. It's the eve of Jesus' birthday, and in all my life I've never felt a part of Christmas like I do now. Not only knowing, but feeling the meaning of Christmas. The birth of our Lord and Savior, who still does miracles. The reason He came. The will of His Father. Every verse in the Bible is alive in me this season. Alive and well. Alive and for the world to see, so they may believe.

The truth is God has the final say. I may not be able to do the impossible, but He can.

CHAPTER 7

PUTTING THIS CAR
BACK IN DRIVE

*Trust the Lord with all your heart; do not depend
on your own understanding.*

Proverbs 3:5 NLT

● ● ● ● ● ● ● ● ● ● ● ● ● ● ●

TRYING TO GET Jayden to have a little sense of urgency, I hollered, "Come on! We've got to go!"

Finally, he was going back to school, and I was going back to work. He was starting middle school during the second semester. We were both rather excited for him to be going to the neighborhood school. This meant he could ride the bus. I felt confident he would make good choices. We had open and honest conversations about many things. But on the first day, I dropped him off myself, got some handsome pictures that I had to beg for, and then watched him walk through those doors into that hallway.

Sixth grade was tough for Jayden. His hair was barely growing back at this point, and he had gotten his first prosthetic leg just four months prior to going to school. Middle school is tough for your average kid. But for a kid with some differences, it's a whole new ball game! He was discovering who he was as an amputee and a survivor of cancer as well as just being a preteen boy. He didn't want people to really know his battle. If they asked, he wouldn't lie, but he would never just come out and say, "I had cancer." No pity parties were allowed on his watch. I'm not sure if he liked me talking about it, but I was just so proud of him that I could not contain my joy and awe of God.

Every day, I thought, "My son was the bravest kid I've ever known."

It wasn't long before Jayden started to get bullied. He was different, and that had never been his circumstance. He was always the funny, athletic, handsome guy. He still was, but other people always focused on his prosthetic leg first, especially middle schoolers who had never seen someone without a leg.

I made it known that I wasn't playing, and Jayden's oncology team wasn't playing either. They were ready to come do a presentation for the whole school. Once I saw the self-inflicted cutting marks on my son's arms, I became a force they did not want to reckon with.

My son had cut himself with me in the room next door, and this did not sit well with me. I could not get over the fact that my child had cut himself—several times might I add—under my roof, without me knowing. I started to question myself as a mother.

There were those stupid lies again: *I am failing at being a mom.*

I called the school and asked the counselor to pull Jayden for a little chat. I wanted to make sure he wasn't suicidal.

"I don't think he is suicidal, but I do think this is a cry for help" the school counselor explained to me, relieving me of the ultimate worry. She promised me that they would keep a close eye on things and not let this go any further.

The week ended with Jayden pushing a kid in PE, letting him and everyone watching know that he was not weak. Jayden had always been strong. His hands were massive, and he had legit anger behind the punches he wanted to throw. He'd had enough of the comments. He'd had enough of them making fun of him for running funny or getting out of breath. So just like that, he pushed the kid so hard he flew into the bleachers. Then, because Jayden was Jayden, he went over to him and helped him up.

Nobody made fun of him after that.

Let me be clear. I do not condone violence, by any means. But we had done everything we could, and it wouldn't stop. Sometimes a bully just needs to be knocked down and helped back up again.

Spring break was a nice, little relief from all the drama at school. I was happy to take a week off, as well. I hadn't worked full time in almost a year, and my body was screaming for some lazy time on the couch. My new job was nowhere near as strenuous as being a teacher, and I was beginning to wonder why I ever wanted to go back. While Jayden was going through treatment, I graduated with my master's degree and passed my state certification exam for school administrators. I just knew I was going to be a principal.

We had a plan. Jayden would go back to school, and I would take some time to heal. I was discovering the trauma I had just been through as a mom and caregiver to a child with cancer. I needed time and space. I would apply for assistant principal positions the following school year, giving myself the rest I thought I needed.

Well, you know what they say; we make plans, and God laughs. That is exactly what happened to me. Three separate times, three different pastors came up to me at church, asking me about my recent graduation with my master's. They were gauging my curiosity about helping start a college campus site at the church. Each time I declined and would tell them my plan.

"Thanks, but I am hoping to be a principal next year."

They each nodded their heads and moved on with the conversation, taking a mental note of my response.

I received a phone call a week or so later.

"Hey Ashley," the family-life pastor said, introducing himself to me. "Several people have brought your name to my attention, I'd like to have you come into my office just to talk."

I knew what he was referring to so there was no need for me to ask. I agreed to meet with him. He sold me on the opportunity, and I was excited to start this new adventure of something I never saw myself doing—working in ministry. I would still be in the education world but with Jesus at the center instead of outside the door.

Shortly after beginning my new job, Jayden got sick. Being back in the pool of germs at school, it was expected. That's when I discovered that I was suffering from Post Traumatic Stress Disorder. Early one morning, I heard the sound of throwing up from Jayden's bathroom, and my whole body almost exploded. My heart leaped from my chest. I threw my comforter to the side, jumped out of my bed, and ran to his bathroom just across the living room of our 1400 square foot apartment.

"Are you okay? What's wrong?" I said in a panic.

"I don't feel good. My stomach hurts." He pushed out the words as he was about to start heaving again. My knees naturally fell to the ground, and my hand started to slide up and down his back, praying for relief. When he was done, I helped him back into bed and took his temperature. There was a slight fever but not enough to call the doctor. I called into work, and Jayden took the day off from school.

By the next day everything was fine. A common, 24-hour stomach bug had terrified me beyond description.

The sound of vomiting was one of my triggers for a very long time. The nausea that happened during treatment wasn't like typical sickness. It was a can't-catch-your-breath, tears-rolling-down-your-face, you-may-pee-or-poop-a-little kind of throwing up. It was gut wrenching to watch. As mothers we want to always be able to fix whatever is going wrong with our children. This was beyond my fix-it reach. The medicine that was given to my child to heal him also made him extremely ill. The internal battle I fought over and over as I watched him go through a variety of side effects was: to continue treatment or not to continue treatment?

Just a few days into our spring break that year, there was news about some pandemic about to take over the world. The world contemplated, the school district contemplated, the church contemplated, and then we were back at home. I was now going to be working from home, and Jayden was going to be doing school from home. COVID-19 had shut down the world.

Being isolated at home was nothing new for us. This was how we had been living our lives for the past nine months. Chemotherapy weakens your immune system to dangerously low levels, and it is safer to avoid crowds. Jayden had his handful of fevers and emergency visits during treatment. Seeing your child in a neutropenic state is scary. Sometimes Jayden wouldn't even be able to hold his head up. This means the common cold is very dangerous to a child during treatment, making socializing with people very difficult. Staying home or only going out during non-peak periods was how we stayed safe then, and how we planned on staying safe now. We learned how to make our home our sanctuary.

I was determined to get Jayden the help he needed to walk this out and learn to love himself again. It just so happened that the hospital had a psychologist on staff to work with the kids, helping them cope with the various stages of this awful disease. Of course, I signed Jayden up. With school being held virtually now, Jayden was able to be his normal, awesome self without any judgments based on things he couldn't control. He started making new friends and keeping in contact with his old friends. He was back to being Jayden again. A funny, full-of-life, charming young man.

Ashley's Journal

March 14, 2020

This year has been full of ups and downs. Last year was hit after hit after hit. And I don't think I've taken the time to recover from my trauma. I feel I am boiling over ... everything is so much to bear on my own. Jayden has his day-to-day struggles, and him being in school has been very stressful! My new job at the church is great, but I miss teaching! I feel I'm not doing enough at my new job. Working out again has been good, but I feel like I am doing it for the wrong reasons at times. Dating has taken up more space in my mind than I would like. I wonder if I am ready for what I want?

"The Lord is my shepherd, I shall not be in want."

Psalm 23:1 NASB

My life was a constant push and pull against the two worlds living inside of me and all around me. I wanted to do good. I wanted to be close to God. I didn't want to sin. I wanted to be changed. I wanted to live out the Christian life. I wanted to be more like Jesus.

On the verge of turning 30, I felt compelled to make better decisions and bigger goals. My journal entries were all about working out and trying to stay healthy but sliding back every 30 days or so. My dating life just seemed to be the same sad story over and over again. I wanted to do good but didn't know how, and of course all my worries about Jayden were always on my mind.

Loneliness and pandemics don't mix well. Thank goodness neither of them last forever.

Jayden's scans had been clear for six months after our Christmas miracle. Enough time had gone by, and the doctors were comfortable with Jayden getting his port taken out. It was a huge relief and a huge victory. Removal of the port meant no more treatment because there's no more cancer. The next step is remission. Due to COVID, a negative test and isolation at home for three days prior to the port removal surgery was required.

The surgery was early in the morning, and we were home by the afternoon. Day surgeries were our favorite, when we didn't have to be admitted to the hospital. We loved the nurses like our own family, but we would rather be home in our own space. And so Jayden added his newest "trophy" to his shelf of accolades: a medically sealed bag with a silver port in it.

It was a trophy symbolizing a victory only God could have given him.

CHAPTER 8

PUTTING THIS CAR
IN REVERSE

*Yet God has made everything beautiful for its own
time. He has planted eternity in the human heart, but
even so, people cannot see the whole scope of God's work
from beginning to end.*

Ecclesiastes 3:11 NLT

● ● ● ● ● ● ● ● ● ● ● ● ● ● ●

I WAS ON the verge of losing it. My best friend Stefanie locked eyes
with me and just knew. She knew I had been waiting for scan results
and must have just received them at work.

"I've got to go!" I said, frantically grabbing my laptop, notepad,
pen, and cup, turning towards the door to exit as quickly as possible.

I wasn't able to get far before all the women who were in the
meeting came filing out the door behind me. I was at a loss for words
and began to wail. My heart was breaking all over again. Jayden's
nine-month scans had shown a couple spots on his right lung. My
co-workers surrounded me while I cried and they just prayed. I just

wanted to run away, to get out of there, but God wanted me to know I was covered and cared about.

I had to go home and tell Jayden the news. Shifting my focus from my feelings to Jayden's helped me calm down and collect myself. When I got home I told him. He was hurt, angry, upset, overwhelmed, and scared. Jayden felt all the emotions, and I gave him the space to do so.

"Am I still going to be able to do the commercial for Scottish Rite Hospital?" he asked. He had been chosen to star in their 100th Anniversary commercial, honoring their years of caring for patients. Jayden had charmed and wowed many professionals and doctors at Scottish Rite. His determination was unmatched, something they hadn't experienced before. Jayden had received his first prosthetic in September of 2019 and his first running leg in February of 2020. He was an athlete whether he had two legs or one.

Ashley's Journal

August 11, 2020

Heartbroken.

Overwhelmed.

Pissed.

Ashamed.

Desperate.

Nine-month scans were yesterday, and the report was not good today. We have an appointment tomorrow morning to get more imaging done. I am praying that there is nothing, but he gave me a 12mm measurement. That scares me! I am heartbroken by this news. I am overwhelmed with emotions because I want my faith to be strong. I am pissed because I am so over this cancer battle, and I want to move on from it. I want Jayden to move on from it! I am ashamed because of the feelings of doubt I am having and the desire to be with a man right now to comfort me instead of the Lord. I am desperate because I don't want to go back to the hospital, a place of uncertainty and death.

We attended a funeral for one of Jayden's friends from the oncology floor last month. We found out yesterday another really good friend is on hospice. He has another friend where the cancer traveled to his brain. It's just all so much for him, and me! This is such a dark place, but with light shining through. When I came home today a hot mess, Jayden started telling me not to worry because God brought him this far and isn't going to leave him now! I believe this! I want so badly to! I spent some time in worship. God help us! Save my son!!!

Trigger tears.

Later for now!

Surgery was scheduled for the following week, two days after my 30th birthday. I was extremely grateful I didn't have to spend my birthday in the hospital. Instead, I got a "COVID car parade!" The world made many adjustments to adapt to the new way of living post-pandemic. One of those adaptations was a carpool-like parade. Family and friends would decorate their cars, buy gifts, and line up to drive by, making a huge ruckus to celebrate you the best they could without hugging you or going into your house. It was special, and I loved it!

My smile always found a way to escape my mouth. Even though our circumstances were at a low, I was able to see the joy and God's hand all over my life. Our community—all the people God had placed in our lives over the years—took us under their wing. I was doing it by myself but I was not alone. Bills were being paid, gifts were being sent over, meals were being placed freshly at our door, cards were being delivered with hand-written encouragement inside, and most importantly, prayers were being prayed all over the nation.

Being back in the hospital after nine months away felt like failure. Everything came rushing back and was all too familiar. There was also somewhat of a new nursing staff and new COVID rules that we had a really hard time abiding by. No one was walking the hall or laughing together in the playroom like they had been before. None of the kids went into each other's rooms to play games or just catch up on life. There was a piece missing—the family piece.

Jayden had only been 12 for one month when he had his second thoracotomy. We knew better what to expect this time—a couple-hour surgery, pain when breathing, the chest tube, and no coughing or sneezing. And that is exactly what it was. There was a two-hour surgery, a spot removed, a chest tube, and pain. By day three, Jayden was up and moving around better. The chest tube was out on day four, and we were home by day five. Five days later he was shooting the commercial for Scottish Rite.

The follow up with the oncologist included talk of a clinical trial. I could not wrap my brain around the fact that we were doing experimental medicine now, that there were no more other approved drugs for my son to take.

The doctor explained the new chemo pills to Jayden and me. He told us how to take them, when to take them, what might happen when you take them, and what they are supposed to do when you take them.

I felt it necessary for Jayden to hear all the information because I wanted him to be able to ask all his questions. After all, he was the one having to endure all of this.

Of course his only question was, "Am I going to lose my hair?"

Without skipping a beat, the doctor said, "There is no guarantee."

We agreed to the clinical trial chemo pills and started right away.

It was a plus not to be admitted to the hospital for treatment. Jayden would do virtual learning from home for 7th grade as his hair slowly fell out and rashes started covering his body. The chemo pills were no easier than the IV treatments he was used to getting.

In the midst of it all, Jayden was given a wish from the Make-a-Wish Foundation, and he got to meet Odell Beckham Jr., his favorite NFL wide receiver. Even though their meeting was virtual, it was still so cool for Jayden. He was completely starstruck by talking to a professional football player. We also got picked up in Jerry Jones' bus to watch the Dallas Cowboys versus the Pittsburgh Steelers game from the perfect view of a suite. We had always been Steelers fans so it was a dream come true. While there were some pretty terrible lows during that time, there were also some incredible highs.

Jayden's next set of scans were mid-November, and the results were not what we were hoping for.

Another lie: *I am not praying enough. I am not doing enough.*

The lies always seemed louder during trouble, making it harder to hear God's voice. I cried out for His help.

Radiation was now being mentioned as a possible treatment. I had no idea what radiation was or what the side effects would be. I needed a consultation.

"There is one big risk," the radiation oncologist said, after handing me a folder, filled with information about how precise the treatment is, what strength they would be using, and how many treatments it was going to take. "The spot is about a centimeter away from his heart. There is a possible risk of damage to his heart."

"Thank you for this information. I am going to go home and pray about it. I'll let y'all know by next week." We left the office, and Jayden and I both buckled in that car and looked at each other. We already knew we didn't like the sound of what he was saying. It was time now to consult our surgeon for yet another thoracotomy.

Because it was Thanksgiving week, some miscommunication and our surgeon being out of town meant it had been a month, and there was still no surgery date. They decided to do another scan before scheduling anything. In the cancer world, waiting is the hardest thing to do. You are dealing with the number one killer of children, and you're told to wait. Not cool.

We rang in 2021 with an appointment for scans. I had been worried for weeks, sick to my stomach, not knowing what was happening inside my precious boy.

"Well, we've been looking at the scans and we aren't 100% sure it is a tumor." The oncologist told me over the phone. The lungs can be tricky when it comes to scans. Dust, scar tissue, leftover stuff from the flu or COVID can show up. Sometimes it's just hard to tell. I was so glad I decided not to do radiation. I called Jayden's surgeon.

"We won't be able to tell without a biopsy, but it's best if I am able to go in there and feel it."

I trusted what he was saying. He had been doing this for decades, and he knew how hard Jayden was fighting this unfair disease. I went ahead and scheduled surgery for a third thoracotomy.

Again we had our expectations: about a two-hour surgery, pain when breathing, a chest tube, and no coughing or sneezing for a while. The surgery went fine, everything was the same as before, except for one minor detail. Jayden had a slight air pocket in his lung called a pneumothorax. I was told it was common with a chest tube and should be absorbed into his body within a couple of days.

Jayden was in a lot of pain. This was the third time they cut into the same place, tearing the same scar tissue, taking out the same lung. His breathing was shallow. He was in and out all day long into the night. There was no getting comfortable for Jayden, and around 2 a.m. things went south quickly.

Jayden's lung collapsed.

He wasn't breathing well, and it looked like his heart was about to pump right out of his scar! I was silently freaking out on the inside while they notified the on-call surgeon. Things were really scary for about two hours, as they were prepping Jayden for emergency surgery.

The surgeon had me step out of the room with her to discuss what was about to happen when the nurse suddenly called us back into the room.

Jayden's stats and breathing were back to normal. They called for another x-ray, which confirmed his lung was indeed inflated again and working properly.

"It fixed itself," the on-call surgeon said, with pep in her voice.

I was amazed, *Thank You Jesus! I know that was You!*

But the following night wasn't much better. Our room had a leak and started raining on us at 3 a.m., and we had to move down the hall.

It was a nicer, bigger room with a better view, but I still had a hard time appreciating it. I was running way below empty at that point.

Eight days went by, and Jayden's chest tube finally got pulled. The protocol was to wait four hours for a post-pull x-ray then you can go home, but because of all the complications Jayden was having, they wanted to keep him overnight.

Right after dinner he started to complain about some pain. They gave him some meds, and we went about our night.

As soon as I asked him to get ready for a shower, the pain started to creep its way back in. More meds were given, but the pain was worsening. None of us knew what was going on.

"Mom, if I go to sleep tonight, I am going to die." Jayden looked me square in the eyes, and there was only seriousness in his voice.

I understood, and went to the nurses' station. I told them what Jayden told me, and they called the doctor. An x-ray was ordered and showed a tension pneumothorax growing inside of Jayden. The air pocket was now growing and pushing on his heart. Jayden was filling up with air.

He had to have an emergency surgery. They placed another chest tube and got the air out. Jayden came back to the room singing and saying hello to all the little green and yellow monsters all around him. He was definitely feeling much better.

"There's got to be a hole in him!" the surgeon said plainly. "I need to go back in, find it, sew him up, and get y'all home."

We scheduled a fourth thoracotomy.

The surgeon found the hole. The tumor he had removed was on the bronchial. When he had shaved it off, it must have thinned the lining of the vessel. Then when Jayden's lung collapsed, it probably stressed the spot enough to tear a hole.

The truth of the matter is that everything came back to God's faithfulness. While the lies wanted me to feel like I was in control, the truth was I never had control. Faith is trusting God and His plan.

Nine more days went by.

Finally, we went home, and Jayden was cancer free, yet again.

CHAPTER 9

TRAINING IS BACK IN SESSION

Work miracles for us, Lord, as You did in the days when You brought us out of Egypt.

Micah 7:15 GNT

● ● ● ● ● ● ● ● ● ● ● ● ● ● ●

"COME ON MOM, I really want a dog!" Jayden begged. He was recovering, and I started to feel like a dog might be good for him. Not a big dog with big poop, but maybe a smaller dog with a big personality. My friend's sister had just rescued a little puppy who was tied to a park bench in the snow. He was house broken and cage broken—two of my requirements.

"We will do a seven-day free trial. I am not making any promises, but we will try," I explained to both Jayden and my friend. I had to make sure Jayden knew this wasn't a yes, but I would put forth the effort. I had always grown up with a dog and loved each of them. I knew this would be good for our family. I just had to get over the fact that I was taking on another very real responsibility.

Chico was perfect. His size. His temperament. His big ears and curly tail. We fell in love before we even reached day three! I made an appointment with a vet, and it was official. I was now a dog mom. I had thought for sure something was wrong with him because who would just leave a perfectly healthy dog to fend for himself? As it turns out, he was very well taken care of and healthy.

"Unfortunately, we have been seeing a number of abandoned dogs since more and more people are resuming life after COVID" the vet told me. During the shut down, people were lonely, shelters and pet stores emptied out only to quickly fill up a year later when the responsibility of normal life and a puppy didn't mix.

We registered Chico to be Jayden's companion, and they instantly were "brothers," playing one minute and screaming/barking at each other the next. Chico came to the hospital with us and quickly became the mascot of the pediatric oncology floor. God, without a doubt, had sent us an angel pup.

Scans were clear at the beginning of March and again at the end of April. More relief had come. Jayden got two new legs in June. One was for walking, and one was for running. His first prosthetic had lasted two years, and his first running leg had lasted about sixteen months. I began to wonder how many legs we were going to go through as he continued to grow like a typical preteen boy.

Normalcy found its way into my life. I was enjoying my job, doing something new and different, as well as working on my healing. Therapy and an amazing women's retreat were pivotal for my healing. My job gave me purpose outside of being an oncology mom and all the hats that came with that. It was fulfilling to help other people discover their calling and help steer them in the right direction. Therapy gave me a safe place to dump it all out and receive tools to help me grow into the woman I was becoming, into the woman God was calling. My experience at the women's retreat connected me with God on a deeper level, in a way I had never known Him before. My prayer closet became my morning command station, a sacred place only He and I would go.

Jayden had an x-ray back in January, prior to his thoracotomy, because he had been complaining of some knee pain in his good knee. With his history, the oncologist thought it was better to be safe than sorry. His exact words to me at our appointment were, "I would be shocked if the cancer jumped to the other side of his body."

Jayden had his x-ray and got to teach the x-ray tech student several things she had never done before. His x-rays were much different and more extensive than your normal broken bone or sprained ankle. We tried to view every part of this battle as an opportunity to do something for someone else, to see God's hand in our every step.

"The x-ray is clear. The pain Jayden is describing and its location could be tendonitis. We suggest you follow up with your orthopedic." We did just that, and Jayden was scheduled for eight weeks of physical therapy.

Your tendons are what connect your muscles to your bones. It is possible to severely injure yourself by tearing a tendon, and that is what we didn't want to happen. Tendonitis is the inflammation or irritation of your tendons caused by overuse or repetitive movements. Rest and physical therapy help to strengthen the tendon, improve flexibility, and recover movement.

Jayden became more flexible and stronger in physical therapy, and eight weeks turned into 12. He needed more rest than anticipated. Upon his graduation of physical therapy, he was upgraded to Scottish Rite's Bridge Program where they take athletes from physical therapy to performance ready. Jayden started participating in personal training three days a week, and before I knew it, he was becoming a well built teenage boy! He trained all summer, gearing up for 8th grade athletics. I had decided to allow him to go to school in person, and he was ecstatic. Everything was going smoothly.

Scans of his lungs were clear in July, and we celebrated his 13th birthday with a "yes day." Whatever Jayden wanted that day—within reason—I said yes. Donuts, yes! A new camera, yes! A photo session, yes! A trip to the electronics store, yes! Lunch at his favorite burger place, yes! A movie with mom, of course, yes!

In August, we took a trip to South Padre Island with some friends who had become family over the years. We had a blast on the beach and explored the island. Jayden was having a blast!

I didn't expect that to change so quickly.

"I'm pretty sure I broke my leg," Jayden told me nonchalantly. I turned to him with a confused look on my face because he was walking toward me as he was saying this. "I was building a sand castle. Then it just fell on my leg, and I felt a pop."

"But you're walking ..." I was trying to make sense of what I was seeing and hearing.

Later, I could tell he was probably right when I started noticing he had to take breaks from walking around. We were at the sea turtle rescue center, and he had to sit down every few minutes or so. His excitement was fading, and pain was kicking in. I knew I would have to schedule an appointment when we got back home. This time, I went straight to our orthopedic because this was just a broken bone. It took about a week for an appointment to open up.

We were scheduled for an x-ray on my birthday, but the news we received was anything but a gift.

"I'm sorry, but it's back. This time it's in the right femur and his pelvis from what I can see on these x-rays." Our orthopedic had to break the news to us. It was clear that they didn't have to do this often because everyone in the room had tears welling up in their eyes as Jayden cried. I stood up from my chair and swallowed the lump in my throat as I went to go hug my boy. I knew he was feeling defeated and scared.

Thank goodness our doctors, nurses, techs, secretaries, security, and all employees of the hospitals we went to became friends and family. The communication and appointments were all done for us. Everyone felt the sting of this relapse. Statistics were not in our favor, and this skip-metastasis relapse was something new the pediatric oncology world was experiencing with osteosarcoma.

We scheduled another port surgery, because Jayden was going to be starting chemo again soon. This time it would be with a new drug that is considered a second-line treatment for spreading throughout the bones—ifosfamide. I made a call to MD Anderson Cancer Research Hospital in Houston for a second opinion. They advised me they would do the same chemo treatment regimen.

Instead of starting his 8th grade year, Jayden was admitted to the hospital to endure five 24-hour bags of chemo. His hair fell out quickly this time, and he was back in his wheelchair. Cancer started stealing from us again, and I couldn't believe God was allowing it to happen.

Ashley's Journal

August 20, 2021

Today life feels like it is moving in the wrong direction. Jayden is getting a port placed again and starting chemo. Lord, please we need a miracle, I need You to rise up and show Yourself mighty on my son's behalf! Make his dry bones come to life! Revive his body! Restore his health!! I thank You and praise You for the miracle and testimony my son will have for Your Kingdom's sake. I pray You give us strength as we wait on You! Thank You Lord for never leaving us. Thank You for being in control! I love you Lord! HEAL MY BOY! YOUR SON NEEDS HEALING!

August 25, 2021

Lord, we need a miracle! You gave me a promise: Jayden would run and not grow weary, that he would walk and not fall. (Isaiah 40:31) I believe You for it! Lord, I need You to come through for my son. He is Your son first! I know You see him hurting! I know You hear what they are telling me. Help! We need a miracle! You can do it Lord, I believe! Jayden shall live and not die. Dry bones LIVE! Allow him to keep his bones Lord. Thank You for hearing my prayers. Thank You for a healing miracle. Let all the world see Your power and know You alone are Lord. I love You!

My prayers became desperate, and I would cry out to the Lord multiple times a day. He gave me a promise, and I stood on it. I would write it on Jayden's mirror and tell him to read it out loud every day. As he sat in his wheelchair looking up at the verse on the mirror he would say the words. My prayer was that as he kept repeating the Word of God over himself, he would start to believe, and we would both see the promise of God happen before our eyes.

I believed the words God spoke to me in my prayer closet. I believed that Jayden was going to walk again. I believed we would see dry bones come back to life.

What do we do when we believe? We take steps of faith. I started meeting with Jayden's school to work out a plan for him to go back to school in person.

Even though Jayden was in a wheelchair, and his hair was falling out, going to school was a big deal for him. He wanted to be with his friends. I could understand that so I did what I had to do to make it happen. He would get to go back to school, but not before we had another scare at the hospital.

This time it was deadly tumor fever.

CHAPTER 10

PRAYING FOR A MIRACLE WHILE EVERYONE IS PLANNING A FUNERAL

... but they who wait for the Lord shall renew their strength; they shall mount up with wings like eagles; they shall run and not be weary; they shall walk and not faint.

Isaiah 40:31 ESV

● ● ● ● ● ● ● ● ● ● ● ● ● ● ● ● ●

THE WORD "HOSPICE" hung in the air as soon as it came out of the doctor's mouth. I couldn't bear hearing it. All the life was sucked out of me, and I began to grieve yet again for everything my son had been through.

Home from the first round of the new chemotherapy for a little over a week, we thought the fever was a side effect. We were still learning this new drug and how it affected Jayden. But it wasn't just the chemo, as we had hoped. All the tests for viral infections had come back negative, as well as the cultures for bacterial infections. Doctors had ruled out all other possibilities for the fever. We learned that Jayden had developed something called tumor fever. The tumor in his now dying femur was causing him to have a fever, making his body sick.

The femur is fairly important for the body as a whole. Your femur bears the weight of most of your body while you're standing and moving. It is a major part of the skeleton, helping us maintain posture and balance. Being the longest bone in your body, a large portion of bone marrow is created in the femur, which helps produce blood cells. Injuries to femurs are often immobilizing.

"We think chemo will help Jayden feel better. We will start his next round as soon as we can get the meds," the oncologist told me during his rounds a few days after we had been admitted. Jayden had been in so much pain, we needed to do something to help stop the pain and keep that fever gone. He started on his second cycle of ifosfamide, another five 24-hour bags of chemo.

The orthopedic surgeon who had done Jayden's amputation surgery came by to give us his opinion. He asked me to step out of the room with him.

"In order to get rid of the cancer, a very serious amputation would have to take place. We would have to go through his pelvis and take the whole right leg. This would change almost everything about his life, including how he eats and uses the bathroom."

For a moment, it was hard to breathe.

I knew Jayden would rather die than become completely dependent on me to take care of his every need. "If you think that taking half of my son's body is going to make him want to fight this thing, you don't know him very well."

"I know Jayden is a very active boy, I just had to give you all of your options at this point."

"Thank you. We will start chemo and hope for the best." Jayden's quality of life was way more important to me than getting rid of the cancer. We were all now on the same page.

By the time bag five was hung, I had noticed Jayden slurring every other word and losing his balance. At one point, his hands started to shake uncontrollably, and he couldn't hold his water to drink it. The chemo was stopped, and he started to get back to his usual self by morning.

After a 10-day stay in the hospital, we were back home, trying to get into a much-needed routine. Jayden was going to do school from home for a little bit longer, and I called upon my "village" to stay with him a couple days a week so that I could go into the office. Work was a nice break for me, but I was constantly worrying and checking in with Jayden. Of course, every time he would tell me, "I'm fine, mom. Don't worry!"

I wasn't a total helicopter mom, but I did keep a close eye on my son. We were fighting a spiritual battle just as much as we were fighting a physical battle. Anything could happen. I was on guard, interceding daily for my household. I would pray for God to stand guard at our door and go before us each day. Knowing that the Creator of the Universe was by my side gave me the confidence I needed to continue moving forward, one step at a time.

Finally, the fever went away. Jayden recovered and was ready to go to school. I never imagined my child begging me to go to school, but when this simple routine of youth is taken away from you for so long, you tend to miss it. After every summer break, what are kids excited to do? Go back to school to see their friends. That's all Jayden wanted, too. With a backpack on his back and his wheelchair in the trunk, it was time for 8th grade to start.

That was our reality.

My son was on hospice with cancer in his leg, and he was going to school like nothing was wrong. Nobody but my family and close friends knew Jayden was on hospice. The words could barely leave my mouth. I was fighting with my reality and faith every day, sometimes every hour. I struggled with balancing the reports from the doctors and what God promises in His Word. I was seeking Him and diving deep into my Bible daily. My appetite was bottomless. I was a student—a disciple—and God was my teacher, sharing with me the secrets of His Kingdom.

I believe the Word of God. I believe God is who He says He is. I believe in Jesus Christ His Son and the Holy Spirit. I believe He is the same yesterday, today, and tomorrow. I believe He still does miracles; I've seen it happen! That is what made what I was experiencing as confusing as if I were hitting a brick wall of unbelief.

My prayer during this horrid season was the vision Ezekiel had at the valley of dry bones (Ezekiel 37:1-14). Elevation Worship released a song called Rattle during that time, and it was based on this passage in Scripture as well. Ezekiel the prophet is taken to a valley of dry bones. God asks him if the dry bones can live, and he responds to the Lord that only He knows. God then commands Ezekiel to prophesy to the dry bones that they may live.

Obeying the Lord, Ezekiel prophesies to the bones, and they start to rattle as they connect to make skeletons. The prophet looks again to see that the bones now have muscles and tendons growing around them. Then they were covered with a layer of skin. But they still had no breath. He prophesies again, and breath was breathed into the bodies, allowing them to stand up on their feet as a vast army, ready for battle.

Dry and dead to alive and well.

I would read this story over and over again, visualizing Jayden's bone coming back to life. I could see him walking around the house once again. This passage in Scripture became my battle cry, and the song Rattle became my anthem, as I held on to the promise God had given me.

Jayden will run and not grow weary. He will walk and not fall.

In the midst of all that was happening, our beloved pastor, Pastor Ricky Texada, passed away from COVID. When we found out Jayden had relapsed on my birthday, Pastor Ricky had called me from his hospital bed to encourage me. He reminded me who I was and who Jayden was.

"Meditate on Romans 8:2, and I'm praying for you guys. Tell Jayden I'm thinking about him," he said as we hung up the phone.

Then he went into a coma, never to wake up again on this side of eternity. I thought about that phone call often, wondering if his very last phone call was to encourage a single mom whose one and only son was just given terrible news. That sounds just like Pastor Ricky.

During the funeral, Jayden was at home with a report of death hanging over him. I tried so hard not to picture Jayden's funeral during Pastor Ricky's, but the thought kept haunting me. I could see it clear as day—my son in the casket and not Pastor Ricky. I tried to shake the madness from my thoughts and focus on honoring the life I had come there to celebrate.

We had scans in mid-October. At this stage in the game, Jayden was getting full scans every two months. It was a lot, and it sometimes took two full days at the hospital, but we all needed to know what was happening inside Jayden's body. This very aggressive, very unpredictable disease required constant monitoring.

The scans came back looking "a million times better," according to the oncologist and orthopedic surgeon. Two months of aggressive chemo had started shrinking the tumors in his bones. God had heard our prayers. Could this be another miracle in the works? My heart danced within me, as I thanked God for what He was doing.

By November, Jayden was up and out of his chair walking. He was discharged from hospice. God had kept His promise! I saw God's Word come alive through Jayden. Once there was an x-ray of a dead bone, a cancer-withered bone, and then there was an x-ray of a bone with new life, new growth. Dry bones really do come alive when they hear the Word of the Lord!

December was quickly approaching, and we were praying to see yet another Christmas miracle in Jayden's life. The medical staff was already very impressed with Jayden's progress. They were our second family, and they all wanted to see Jayden beat this thing.

He finished his sixth cycle of chemo at the beginning of that month and then received another set of good scans a few weeks later. The cancer was continuing to shrink as Jayden continued to live his life, loving school and loving people. Everyone wanted to be around because his light was shining so bright. And every day I would wake up proud to be Jayden Xavier Simmons's mom. He was becoming a responsible and mature young man of God.

By just living and doing the things he loved, Jayden inspired those around him. They would see him stopping to pick up trash or taking the time to greet an elderly lady and make her smile. That made others want to make someone's day better, too.

His presence was contagious. His laugh, his encouragement, his jokes, and his grit marked him as someone anyone could be around. From babies to adults, people loved Jayden and his spirit. He made the world a better place. With Jayden around, it was never a dull moment, and there was never a face without a smile on it.

CHAPTER 11

PUSHING CHEMO
TO THE MAX

Now our hope for you is unshakable, because we know that
just as you share in our sufferings you will also share in
God's comforting strength.

1 Corinthians 1:7 TPT

* * * * * * * * * * * * * * *

"WHAT DO YOU think about doing maintenance chemo with ifos?"
our oncologist asked us. "He seems to be responding really well, and
since we have lowered the concentration, I think we can get some
maintenance cycles in. Instead of five bags every 21 days, we will do
three bags every 28 days." We both looked over to Jayden because it
was his turn to give the final approval.

"I'm fine with that," he said shrugging one shoulder towards his
chin in a very chill manner.

Jayden started the first maintenance cycle about a week later.
Our new year was starting off with some certainty and routine, a nice

change from the previous year. Hospital stays would only be three or four days instead of five or six. Two days less would make time fly by.

I had become a professional at packing for the best experience at the hospital. I would refer to our time in the hospital as a chemo party, insinuating that we were going to have loads of fun. First and foremost was our comfort. I would pack everything Jayden liked for his bed, which was two soft blankets, two regular size pillows, and a small pillow to prop up his head. For me, I would almost pack an entire twin bed set: a blanket for on top of the fitted sheet, a king size pillow, a quilt, and another blanket in case Jayden decided 50 degrees was a good temperature for our room. The chemo often made him abnormally warm.

All of our entertainment was essential because, let's face it, you never know what could happen and how long you could actually be at the hospital. Jayden wanted his firestick every time but his video game station only sometimes. The chemo had a tendency to make his hands shake, which would cause him to lose whatever game he was playing. That would provoke anger, and sometimes he just didn't want to deal with that. Quite frankly, neither did I.

There was a season when we always had a few toy guns with us, too. That would lead to wars after midnight and a nice little "put your hands up" every time someone came into our room. I had a library of books and a couple puzzle options for myself. We dare not get bored.

The entire trunk of my car would be full, everything placed perfectly in order to fit just right. A giant suitcase, refrigerated food, pantry food items, drinks, entertainment, bedding, and all our everyday needs came with us. Each hospital stay we would wholeheartedly move into our room, making that little corner of the hospital our home. I would anoint the doors, Jayden's bed, and anything else I thought needed some extra Holy Spirit. I believed the hospital and that floor was my territory, our home away from home for almost four years.

When six cycles of maintenance chemo ended, Jayden was thriving. We now understood how this chemo affected him so there weren't any side effects we couldn't handle quickly. Jayden was doing well in school, training with Scottish Rite again, and running a mile in less than ten minutes. My mile is still ten minutes—go figure! Jayden had an appetite for life like no one I had ever seen before.

Not even a marathon runner's stress fracture would slow him down.

"Mom, I think my leg is broken," he said after school one day, rubbing right beneath his knee. This time I had no questions, Jayden knew his body pretty well at this point. I called his orthopedic doctor and let them know. Of course they wanted to know if he was in any pain. I told them that he was walking around, and it would bother him every so often.

Sure enough there was a fracture and rest was prescribed. Jayden smiled when he told his oncologist and nurses about his stress fracture because it was common in marathon runners. This fracture was a proud injury. It showed that Jayden had been training hard. It wasn't because cancer was making him weak.

When May finally rolled around, Jayden was so ready for high school. His 8th grade year had been amazing. God had done something beautiful for Jayden and redeemed middle school. The boys who used to pick on Jayden ended up becoming some of his most protective friends. And because Jayden was wise beyond his years, the staff couldn't get enough of him. His sense of humor was unmatched.

God is a redeemer, and He allows us to see beauty come from the ashes.

We made the decision to hit the pause button on chemo for the summer. I really wanted Jayden to enjoy his summer and not have to worry about hospital stays or surprise fevers.

Summer break began with a trip all around the San Marcos area with the Sunshine Kids. One of Jayden's nurses had recommended him for this once-in-a-lifetime trip. Picture it, a couple dozen kids who are fighting cancer or have survived cancer exploring Texas, going on police-escorted shopping sprees, riding on the back of motorcycles, floating the river, and running around a hotel with kids who just "get it." I received pictures throughout the week he was gone, and my heart burst with joy to see the smiles and adventures.

Jayden came back home with a tan and was simply glowing. I knew right away that he'd had a camp crush, a little summer fling! He had kissed her but nothing else. I was relieved! My son was a good boy. He loved Jesus!

Next, we spent time on both Lake Hawkins and Lake Ray Hubbard with friends and family. Jayden's tubing skills were out of this world. Meanwhile, I got splashed in the face with nasty lake water and kept praying my contacts wouldn't fall out.

"I can't see!" I yelled, spitting out water at the same time.

Jayden laughed and reached a hand over to wipe my eyes. I couldn't help thinking, How did I get so lucky? My son is so considerate.

The next getaway was a week of youth camp—together! I worked in the youth ministry at the time and was considered the "Legendary Mom." I was the "mom" of the group. I made sure everyone knew the rules and followed them. Not much slipped past me, and Jayden finally learned it was just better to be honest.

Camp was fun. Camp was wild. Camp was hot!

And I wouldn't have traded a minute of it.

For his fourteenth birthday, Jayden wanted a nice birthday dinner with his family and his best friend at a local steakhouse. It was simple but so very special. Ever since our experience with cancer began, it seemed like each birthday got more special, more meaningful. I offered to do something fun with his friends, and he said yes to paintballing.

We attended several weddings that summer. Jayden humored me by wearing a matching outfit to one of them, and our pictures turned out great. After so many weddings, people started joking that Jayden was my "plus one." I didn't mind at all.

We went roller skating, and Jayden figured out how to do it with a prosthesis. We signed the waiver for a person with a broken leg that has a cast, rented our skates, and were on our way. Jayden had one roller blade on his right foot and used his prosthetic leg to push off the left side and start rolling, almost like riding a scooter. There was never a challenge he didn't face head on.

The cherry on top of our perfect summer was that Jayden got to experience a normal first day of school like all the other kids. There hadn't been a normal first day of school since he was in fifth grade. Who knew that the first day of school could be such a highlight for a ninth grade boy and his mom.

He enjoyed a couple predictable weeks before maintenance chemo started back up again. I was trying to keep his life as normal as possible so we checked into the hospital on a Friday afternoon, right before the doctor's office closed. This allowed Jayden to be in school for the majority of the day rather than missing too much school. It was a blessing to have everyone on our team working to ensure Jayden got to live his best life.

The first bag of maintenance chemo went as expected. But as bag two was hung that evening, something happened that we'd never seen before.

I had just made some lavender tea, and we were getting ready for bed when Jayden started to have a seizure. A code was called for him, and within minutes, our room was flooded with doctors, nurses, techs, and the surgeon on call.

Jesus! Jesus! Jesus! What is happening? Make it stop! Please God, please! What have I done?

The seizures lasted for about an hour, and chemo was stopped. Jayden's body told us it had had enough.

I sunk into my chair that night, overwhelmed with guilt and a brand new lie: I should have known better.

CHAPTER 12

HIGH SCHOOL AND HIGH STANDARDS

Little children, you can be certain that you belong to God and have conquered them, for the One who is living in you is far greater than the one who is in the world.

1 JOHN 4:4 TPT

● ● ● ● ● ● ● ● ● ● ●● ● ● ● ●

"WHY DID I get an email from your teacher saying you were being disruptive in class today, and it has progressively been getting worse?" I asked Jayden, even though I already knew that he was going to say he didn't do anything.

"And before you say 'I didn't do anything,' I want you to think long and hard because I will call a meeting with your teacher."

He knew I was serious.

"All my friends are in that class, and it's hard to focus. I need my ADHD medicine."

I appreciated his honesty.

"Do you have assigned seats?"

"No." He knew where I was going with this.

"Then find somewhere else to sit, somewhere you can focus and complete your work." I gave him this option because we both knew that the next email would come with a hefty consequence. "Let's try self-control before we put you back on those meds. You've been on so many meds, and I'd like to give your body a break."

"Fine," he said with a slight attitude because he thought I didn't know what I was talking about, that I didn't understand what it is like to have 50 million things rolling around in your mind while trying to focus, that I didn't know what it's like to be a social butterfly. Didn't he realize that he got this trait from me? I am still a social butterfly, just one with self-control.

Could Jayden's behavior have been linked to the fact that he had scans coming up on Friday? Possibly. Could Jayden have been learning how to be a typical student again after being home for three years? Possibly. Could Jayden have been trying to make a name for himself in high school? Possibly.

Because I remembered how his father and I were in high school, I wanted Jayden to know I would be involved with his school. There would be no disrespectful behavior in class or letting his friends distract him. Lord knows, I was all up in his business about everything. I checked his phone regularly, and that is how I found out that he had a potty mouth and a new crush. I emailed his teachers once a month to check in—some were positive while others were disappointing. I always said hi to Jayden's friends, whether they were on the phone, coming off the bus, or passing by. I wanted to know his friends. I wanted to know what was happening in his life.

When I was in high school, I had hidden everything from my parents—my friends, my phone, my boyfriends, and my plans. The lies I told in order to be able to do whatever I wanted still make me feel slimy to this day. I don't know if my parents knew I was lying, but nobody ever checked on me. They trusted me, and I was not a trustworthy teenager.

Jayden was different. He was not good at lying. My favorite lie he ever told was about fruit cups. You know the fruit cups that come in packages of four? I had just gone to the grocery store and purchased two four packs for Jayden. He loved eating the fruit then tilting the cup back to slurp down all the fruit juice. I had taken Chico for a walk, Jayden stayed inside to play a game. When I came back, I saw that three fruit cups were missing.

"Jayden, how many fruit cups did you have while I was gone?" The tone in my voice cued him to think about his response.

"Two!" He said, very sure of himself.

"Are you sure?"

"Yes, I swear I had two!" He took off his headset and made his way into the kitchen where I was standing.

"Can you explain why there are three empty fruit cups in the trash can?"

His eyes lowered. "All right, I ate three."

"Why would you lie to me about that? That is probably one of the dumbest lies. Did you think I wouldn't notice, or that I wouldn't find your trash?"

"I was afraid I was going to get in trouble."

"Well, now you are in trouble, but not for eating three fruit cups. You are in trouble for lying." Jayden's consequence for lying, no matter the lie, was getting his TV taken away. If he just so happened to lie again, the phone was next. "Groceries are expensive and I just went this morning. You've eaten almost a whole pack of fruit cups. If you're hungry, eat some real food."

"Yes, ma'am." He turned to go back to his room with his head hung down. He knew his TV was about to be taken away. Lying was something we had been working on for a while.

My thinking was if he would lie about something small, he would lie about something big. But he never did. All his lies were little ones, hoping he wouldn't get in trouble. All my lies had been big, and my fear was that Jayden would learn how to lie like I had. I knew from experience how getting away with one little lie could turn into a slew of bad choices very quickly.

The Friday after I had received the disciplinary email from his teacher was a full day of scans. Jayden would have a sedated MRI (four hours), get a CT of his lungs (a few minutes), and get injected with dye for his full body bone scan (four and a half hours). A full eight hour day at the hospital. The peak of these kinds of days was going to the pediatric oncology floor to have lunch with the nurses. We loved going to the floor when we weren't admitted. It carried a lighter weight than on admission days.

While we waited for the dye to rush through his veins, making its way to each bone, we would go to the hospital cafe to get pizza or wings. Then we'd head up stairs for lunch in the conference room of the pediatric oncology floor. The nurses would come in as their patient load allowed and spend time catching up with us. Now that Jayden was in high school, the hot topics were school and girls. If the floor wasn't too full, we would get the chance to play a game with them. We were competitive. "Show no mercy" was our family game night slogan.

Later that day, I saw the bone scan. I had seen many bone scans before, and I knew if there was cancer, it lights up the area. I saw almost nothing light up. I left the hospital after that long day with joy and hope in my heart. Something was telling me it was all going to be okay.

Sure enough it was. Jayden was deemed "stable." The bone scan showed very little evidence of disease, and the MRI showed that the tumor could possibly be dead. His lungs were about the same as last time. The news I had been praying for was NED—No Evidence of Disease. It was not the best news, but it wasn't the worst news, either. I knew Jayden would be happy and excited to be going home so that he could go on with school and his social life.

But it wasn't long before the enemy came to attack him again. This time it was with his prosthetic leg and wheelchair. He had received the most basic wheelchair when his leg was amputated— no cushioned seat, no back support. It was a temporary chair, and I thought Jayden would not use it. I was wrong. Around the house, it was easier for him to be in his chair. He rolled around from the kitchen to his room to the living room. He didn't always want to go through the process of putting on his leg—it was quite the process. He had to find the right amount of socks to put under the shell because Jayden's weight fluctuated, due to being on and off chemo. The wheelchair was a must.

Eventually, someone donated a pretty cool chair to him because insurance only allows one wheelchair to be purchased every three to ten years. This chair was bright and colorful with a nice cushion and back support, but what Jayden liked most was its big snow tires. The chair had previously belonged to someone who lived in a snowy area. Jayden loved leaning back and doing wheelies on those snow tires. My one rule was no wheelies at the hospital. All four wheels had to stay on the ground. It was such a good chair, and he enjoyed it. Soon, he'd start growing out of that one, too.

I fought with the insurance company to get a customized wheelchair approved. It can take up to nine months to get a wheelchair. We waited almost a year.

Then his running leg, the leg he wore everyday broke. The hydraulic knee kept making a clicking noise for a few days then it just stopped working. Every time Jayden kicked out his leg to walk, the knee would give out. We reported this to Scottish Rite, and they ordered a new knee right away. It was a blessing that there was still a warranty on it so insurance didn't give us too much of a hassle.

But because of COVID, the supply chains were still completely messed up. We waited longer than we should have for a replacement knee to come in. When it finally came in, the foot on Jayden's prosthetic snapped. We had to wait again. The enemy was overplaying his cards, and we knew it.

As October came to an end, Jayden was due for another set of scans. This time it was only an MRI, and it was only four hours at the hospital instead of eight. We still went to have lunch with Jayden's nurses. They were all "Jayden's nurses," and it was well known.

Once again, the doctors said he was stable. The joy I felt was indescribable. For the first time, I understood how people could be so full of joy that they would run up and down the aisles at church.

We had our first Thanksgiving and Christmas since diagnosis with no worries in the world. Jayden had returned to training three days a week as soon as his leg was fixed. Life was good.

But stability doesn't mean remission, and I began the journey to find a clinical trial.

CHAPTER 13

THE MOUNTAINS OF COLORADO, CANCER, AND CORPORATIONS

I will climb up to my watchtower and stand at my guardpost. There I will wait to see what the Lord says and how He will answer my complaint.

Habakkuk 2:1 NLT

● ● ● ● ● ● ● ● ● ● ● ● ● ● ●

AT THE MID-JANUARY scan report, Jayden's lungs were clear, but there was a mention of a "bone marrow enhancement" in his femur, and I wanted clarification.

"So what does that mean exactly?" I asked the oncologist.

"I believe this is the tumor and possible live cells, but the measurement is small so we aren't going to worry about it just yet. Is Jayden in any pain?"

"No, not at all. He is excited to play sports again." He was fine. He wasn't in any pain. He was doing really well, and that was part of my confusion. The cancer was reappearing and possibly growing, but Jayden was fine. He was walking, running, and working out. How could that be?

"We will send the scans and reports to Scottish Rite and follow up with them about a sports release." The oncologist was okay with Jayden doing anything he enjoyed as long as he wasn't in pain or sick.

As I waited for a call from Jayden's orthopedic, I frantically read over the report again and again, trying to make sense of it all. I looked up the words I had never heard of before and found way more information on the Internet than I wanted to find. When searching for anything that involves childhood cancer, there aren't too many pleasant positive things out there.

I kept praying. I kept believing. Our prayer warriors kept praying and believing.

Jayden's orthopedic called while we were at church on a Wednesday night. Thank goodness we were surrounded by people who loved us and were fighting with us. It was confirmed: Cancer was on the move.

"Please, I have to know. Can Jayden play a sport?" Holding back tears, I had to ask the question because I knew that would be Jayden's one and only question.

"I think it would be good for him, and if he is not in any pain I will release him to play baseball, tennis, or swimming."

"I will be finishing his baseball paperwork tonight! Thank you so much!"

"Please reach out if you need us any further." Our whole team was always going above and beyond for Jayden, making sure he was able to do all he could with their support.

I could not let myself fall apart for a couple more hours. I had responsibilities that night at youth, and I needed to focus. That would have been easier if we weren't like a family. As soon as I turned the corner, people knew. It was written all over my face: worry, sadness, and fear.

Within thirty seconds, I was surrounded by our team. They laid hands on me and began to war and intercede on our behalf. It took everything in me not to sink into the floor and just let it all out. I knew my pain was deep, and my heart was broken. There was no telling what could have come out of my mouth, and I didn't want to scare anyone.

I had been researching clinical trials since Jayden had his seizure incident with the last round of chemo. One was in Seattle, one in Boston, and the other in San Francisco. Between our team and my consultation with an osteosarcoma specialist and researcher, these were the trials they recommended. All of them had different treatments and different protocols, but all "seemed positive." In the clinical trial world there is zero certainty and no reassurance. It is just a "trial." Osteosarcoma hadn't had any new successful drugs come out since the seventies.

Jayden was not quite old enough for the trial in Seattle, Car-T. That trial consisted of the removal of some t-cells from Jayden's body, rewiring these cells to be cancer-fighting cells, and then reinstating the cells back into Jayden's body in hopes that they would multiply and kill off the cancer. Sounds like a dream right? I was interested but had no idea how the logistics of it all would work out.

The trials in both Boston and San Francisco were a mix of different kinds of drugs, some in phase one and some in phase two. I was scared of the phase one trials. This is the phase where they see how much of a drug someone can tolerate. Phase two is where they test out timelines. I wasn't thrilled about traveling to another state for treatment so I was waiting until it was a must.

Now that the cancer was on the move, it was a must. I relooked into the clinical trials. Jayden still wasn't old enough for Seattle but there were now several clinical trials being offered at MD Anderson just four hours away in Houston. I made a few calls, sent a couple of emails, and got the show on the road. Medical history, the most recent scan reports, and insurance information was communicated within a couple of hours. Then I fought with the insurance company to cover out-of-network benefits to try to save my son's life.

"What is the cost out-of-pocket for the initial appointment?" I asked the receptionist. I had very generous friends. My thinking was that I could pay out-of-pocket to get us started and work out things with insurance in the meantime. We had a spot in the trial, and I didn't want to lose it.

"Let me get a statement together for you, and I'll send it through the patient portal." The receptionist told me over the phone.

Two days later I got the quote.

It was $75,000 for the first appointment. My jaw hung open as I blinked to adjust my eyes. The outrageous number was still there. I started calling the insurance company everyday. I started making a fuss. By mid-February I thought I was getting somewhere and quickly realized they were going to be playing hardball.

The doctor we were going to see at MD Anderson was approved, but not the actual facility of the hospital. Without both being approved by insurance, Jayden would not be able to receive treatment.

Ashley's Journal

February 26, 2023

I haven't stopped crying all day. I feel so defeated, overwhelmed with it all. I'm scared. I'm hurting. Lord, I need You. Make a way. I can't do this much longer. Everyone says they are here for me, but I don't feel that way. I wouldn't know what to ask them for, they can't help– only You can! Bills are piling up, the trial seems like it is falling through, and I am struggling being a good mom. This week has been so rough, so hard, so heartbreaking. I don't know what else to do! Help me! Please give my son a long and satisfying life. He can have mine. I hate cancer! I hate how it makes me feel! I hate what it has done to me! Show me how this is for my good because I don't see it right now! I can't see past the no.

Psalms 13

Isaiah 55

Ephesians (whole book)

Trying to not let cancer be all consuming, we took a trip for spring break. The car was packed and loaded as we headed to New Mexico to see the Capulin Volcano. Neither one of us had ever seen a volcano in real life, let alone walked across one. Jayden brought the fancy camera he got for his yes-day-birthday and we took some really awesome photos.

We headed to Colorado the next morning to meet up with some friends who were now family. My car pushed itself all the way up and around those mountains to a beautiful snow village in Alma, Colorado. The snow was several feet deep, and Jayden was in heaven. We had plans to walk some trails, but after Jayden's full day of playing in the snow, his leg needed a rest. I had to constantly remind him to take it easy and slow down.

Because I have learned to be flexible, thanks to the way life has just thrown itself at me, we adjusted our plans to have a spa day with massages and facials. The next day we went to the paralympic museum and had the best time. It became a core memory.

We were on the second level of the museum looking at all the prosthetic legs and athletes who were amputees when a second grade field trip walked in and thought that Jayden was famous. They looked at the legs displayed on the walls, looked down to see his prosthetic, and thought he was an Olympian. Of course Jayden played into it and we had a long laugh that lasted well past our trip.

Baseball season started shortly after we got back home. Right away Jayden fell in love with the sport and his team. Even though most of the team spoke Spanish and had been together for a few seasons, they welcomed us with open arms. I'm sure everyone had their first impressions and questions, but Jayden did his thing and earned the respect of his team. Adding baseball mom to my resume was a proud moment.

Jayden's team ended up only losing two games throughout the season and landed themselves in the championship. We lost by two runs in the final inning, but boy, was it a great game! It was a great season, a God season. Jayden received a championship ring for being a finalist. During the championship award ceremony, Jayden was given many compliments by the other teams and coaches. I was one proud mom. He had hit homeruns and had a handful of outs as a first baseman. His stats were impressive for his first and only season of baseball.

God is faithful; it's a truth I will say a million times a day if I have to. He knows the desires of our hearts, and He cares deeply about each one of His children. I had to reach for God's character because I had nothing else to hold onto.

Jayden's scans in April showed more growth and massive spreading.

I was done, fed up with this game the insurance company was trying to play. My son was relapsing again, and we needed to contain this beast before it swallowed him alive.

I called every day. I got every single piece of paperwork they needed and had the correct doctor's office send it—because heaven forbid if the oncologist sends records and not the PCP. I was still getting nowhere and still being denied. I shared my story on social media and started getting calls from people I knew who knew someone who could help me.

Eventually, I got in contact with Senator Ted Cruz's office. They made a phone call, and magically things started to roll. By mid-May we finally got approval. After five months of phone calls, over 100 hours on the phone, countless trips to all of Jayden's doctors, endless paperwork signed and sent, uncountable tears, and unbelievable stress, Jayden could start a clinical trial.

God brought people into my life to help along the way. He gave me what and who I needed to get where He needed us to go. God will equip you for your calling; you don't have to have it all together for Him to use you.

Jayden's baseball team got together for one last game, but this time it was kickball—parents versus players. The team was practically a family. Everyone was talking about signing up for the fall, and I had to let Jayden's coaches know that we would be heading to Houston for a clinical trial. They had no idea. Their words about my son will forever be treasured. They wished that all their players played like Jayden.

They were amazed at his ability to push himself hard, keeping up with the other kids, all while having a monster growing inside of him.

Two days later Jayden was back in his wheelchair, unable to walk and in extreme pain.

CHAPTER 14

IT WAS ALL A BLUR

*So teach us to number our days that we may
get a heart of wisdom.*

Psalm 90:12 ESV

· · · · · · · · · · · · · · · ·

JAYDEN STARTED THE clinical trial at the beginning of June. He also saw a pain management doctor at MD Anderson and was on more meds than I ever thought possible. All I could do was pray that those drugs would stop cancer from taking my boy. I could slowly see him fading. He was losing his spark. The pain was becoming unbearable.

The tumors were now all the way through his femur, his pelvis, his tibia, his hip, and his lungs. For weeks, Jayden would sit in his wheelchair leaning on his right side bearing no weight on his left hip and lay down on his stomach to take all weight off his lower half. He became extremely sensitive to the touch. He could barely tolerate hugs. His zeal for life was slowly slipping away.

I thought a week at summer camp would be good for him so I dropped Jayden off for a week at Camp iHope. Camp iHope is a place for kids and their siblings who have lived the oncology life. It's a place to be with kids who are just like you. It exists so these precious kids could have a week of feeling normal at summer camp. It was a week to have fun with their nurses and doctors. It was a place to allow laughter and joy to heal them in ways chemotherapy never could.

Our Dallas team hadn't seen Jayden in a couple months because we were being treated in Houston. I thought they might be able to encourage him, and they did.

"I'll get this pain stuff taken care of," Kammie, one of the nurses, reassured me. I trusted her. "He's going to have a great time this week!"

When I went to pick up Jayden at the end of camp, he was smiling, laughing, and telling me stories of his late night shenanigans.

"Yeah, one night we stayed up and at 4 a.m. we had a push up contest!" I was shocked by some of the things I was hearing. Jayden hadn't wanted to leave the house or do anything for so long, and now he was excited about something again.

"I really think we can fix this problem." Kammie told me later. "We had another boy a little older than Jayden in very similar pain. We gave him an epidural pain pump, and it worked miracles. He feels a lot better. Jayden needs one!" She got me connected with a new pain specialist in Dallas, and within a few weeks Jayden had the birthday gift of no pain.

"It's a miracle! Thank You Lord!" he would exclaim over and over as he was able to sit straight up in his chair and lie on his back.

The scans at the end of July showed that the trial was not working. We were given some other clinical trials to look at. Jayden was now 15, making him eligible for Seattle, but then there would be the battle with insurance again. I called our team in Dallas, and we started making a plan.

All of this was so hard to navigate as a mom. There was no book called, What to Expect When Your Child Gets Cancer. I didn't know how to help Jayden. I didn't know how to help myself. I did what I could, making him appointments to see his psychologist and keeping him involved in church where everyone was encouraging him and praying for him.

Jayden had his first day of school at home. We ate lunch, and then it happened. Jayden was unable to go to the bathroom. He started to swell from the belly button down, and developed a slight fever.

We had never experienced this before. This time Jayden was the one freaking out, and I was the one remaining calm. I called the oncologist to let them know, and they admitted us. While I was on the phone with the oncologist, I packed all our bags, arriving at the hospital within the hour.

All the usual things happened, with a few added x-rays and scans. The tumor in Jayden's pelvis was causing problems, pushing on his bladder and colon. The first doctor suggested the idea of an ostomy bag and a catheter. The second doctor pumped the brakes, offering to try one an option that began with a super pubic catheter. We agreed and surgery was scheduled.

While we waited for the cultures to come back and the fever to break, we received scan results.

They were not good. Not good at all. The cancer had grown and spread like wildfire. As the days went on, the news just kept getting harder. They gave Jayden two weeks to six months to live. There is no word in the English language to explain how I was feeling. I couldn't live without my son.

I didn't know what was true anymore. We had seen God do the impossible time and time again for Jayden. We were believing in a miracle and expecting it. I clung to my faith and to who I knew God to be. But there was no denying what was happening, and I didn't want the Lord to prepare me.

I took leave from work and pulled Jayden from school. He would start a new chemo pill just to try to "slow things down a bit." I started filling up our calendar with his favorite things.

First up was a Texas Christian University game. They were playing Southern Methodist University so it was only fitting to go with my brother and sister-in-law. She ran track for SMU, and Jayden planned to attend TCU when he graduated high school. It was a perfect game for Jayden's first time. TCU won, and we left with some gnarly sunburns.

Next was a Steelers game. They were playing the Houston Texans so we took our first trip to Houston that wasn't to a hospital. Again we went with my brother and my sister-in-law. Jayden and my brother were tight, but Jayden and my sister-in-law were like glue! My brother and his wife had been high school sweethearts. I'd had Jayden when I was in high school. We all kind of grew up together.

The game was rough, and we lost horribly. The Houston fans were loud about it, but it was cool to be there, getting a pre-game field experience and seeing JJ Watt, the Texans defensive end, earn his place in the Ring of Honor. We all were starstruck. Cam Heyward, the Steelers defensive tackle, had a conversation with Jayden, and it made his day.

Next, we went to experience Bourbon Street for the first time together. We quickly learned that New Orleans is not an accessible city. The brick sidewalks and roads made it hard for Jayden to transport himself in his chair. It frustrated him because I was not the best pusher. Besides that, the food was awesome, the culture was vibrant, and the people knew how to have fun. Jayden even had a "Warrior's Second Line" down Bourbon Street in his honor. A second line is a parade and a New Orleans tradition. It was a Thursday evening around seven o'clock, and the streets were kind of bare, but when the band started up and the Mardi Gras Indian started walking, people started to line the streets. The city suddenly came out of hibernation.

We walked from the restaurant all the way to Jackson Square. Jayden felt celebrated and seen. People were fist bumping him, saluting him, and patting him on the back. He never liked talking about his battle, but it was nice for adults to express how much they admired him for it.

After about 48 hours in New Orleans, we were ready to hit the beach. We drove to Waveland, Mississippi to unwind and enjoy the water. It always amazes me how calming water can be for the soul. Jayden hung out with the guys and spent lots of time fishing. His smile was bright, and you could see the joy in his eyes.

Next up was Morgan's wedding. Jayden had known her since he was three. We had prayed for her husband for years, and the day was finally here. When Morgan had come down to visit us in Houston during our time at MD Anderson, Jayden had asked if he could give a speech at her wedding. She was delighted. His speech brought tears to everyone's eyes, even his own. It was a beautiful night, one I will never forget.

As we were heading home from the wedding, I noticed swelling like I had never seen before. Jayden's hip, thigh, and ankle had been swollen for a couple of months, but now I was starting to see marks. They looked like deep-red stretch marks. His vessels were finally showing the months of stress. The tumors were cutting off his circulation. There was no way to fix this because essentially the tumors were bone. They were solid and would snap any stent put in his leg. It was excruciating to see, but there was nothing to do but keep living until we just couldn't take another step.

One of the coolest things Jayden got to do during this time was design a shirt with the Dallas Stars for their Hockey Beats Cancer night. Salood, a charity we knew through another family, asked if Jayden would want to do this, and I am so glad he said yes. The experience of working with the Dallas Stars was a dream. The night of the game was far beyond our expectations and Jayden instantly became a Stars fan.

He got to meet every player and coach, shaking their hands and chatting with them before the game. There was also a news crew there, getting content for a story to be run that evening. A few other influencers got footage to post about Jayden's story and experience. They presented him with a custom jersey with the number 17 and his last name on the back. Then we made our way to the ice to have a rinkside seat for their pregame warm up.

The head coach was impressed with Jayden and his story, inviting him to do the locker room roster call that was usually led by the team captain. Jayden's face beamed with excitement as he practiced saying the players names and pausing, giving them time to respond. Finally, we headed up to our suite where we watched the game with our closest friends. It was a night I will cherish forever.

Jayden was happy to be alive each day. When people asked, he would share his story and tell them how he was given two weeks to live. He would share with them about his five-year fight and how many times he had almost died. He was losing basic functions of his body, but his spirit never went to a woe-is-me posture. He was just grateful.

To top it off, Jayden was home for both Thanksgiving and Christmas. We had hoped for home during the holidays for such a long time, and I was determined to make it special.

Of course we went to see his favorite movie, *Elf*, and enjoyed all the holiday goodies.

As we were heading into the new year, Jayden was heading into his final days.

CHAPTER 15

JANUARY 2024

Wake up! Rise to my defense! Take up my case,
my God and my Lord.

Psalm 35:23 NLT

• • • • • • • • • • • • • • • • •

JAYDEN HAD BEEN fighting to breathe for days. With his oxygen machine turned all the way up, his oxygen levels were still at 73 percent. His hospice nurse had come over because Jayden didn't want to go to the hospital anymore; he was afraid he wouldn't come back. With her confirmation I started to pack our bags. Jayden started to cry.

I tried to calm him down the best I could. I didn't want him to struggle and suffer anymore. I assured him that we would come home again if it was the last thing I did. As I packed, I prayed, *Lord, please let my words be true. Bring us back home again. Don't let this be the end. Send Jayden a new pair of lungs. I know You are able, please!*

We headed straight to the pediatric oncology floor, they already had a room ready for us. Jayden got all hooked up and put on oxygen. The respiratory specialist came by to assess the situation. Jayden had

had his right lung drained three days before, removing almost a liter of fluid off his lung.

"I'm not feeling confident with him being on this floor. Have you considered moving to the PICU?" He was kind as he said this but my face must have said I didn't like his idea. "I mean we can better monitor him down there and we have more heavy duty equipment to help with this."

"What did our nurse say?"

"I haven't talked to them yet, but it is my recommendation."

"Please talk with our team and see what they want to do." I know our nurses and doctors like to have their kids, their patients, on their floor. When you move to another unit, other doctors are in charge. We had never been to the PICU, Pediatric Intensive Care Unit, before. Five years of battling cancer, and we had never once been in intensive care.

"Are we going to the PICU?" I asked our nurse when she walked in.

"We are going to try our hardest to keep him here, but if he gets worse you may have to." I knew she saw the worried look on my face. "If he needs another draining procedure they can do it bedside; we can't do that here." She was trying to comfort me, but I didn't know how to take the news.

Jayden got worse throughout the night, and we went to the PICU the following morning. We were devastated. Not only were the rooms in the PICU the size of the bathrooms on the oncology floor, it was a whole new set of staff and doctors, not our family. Our nurses would come see us throughout the day and throughout our time there. There were smiles while they were there and tears when they left.

We wanted to go home. If we were in the PICU, going home wasn't the next step. It would be going back up to the regular floor and then going home.

The days drug onward, and my heart was slowly breaking a little more with each new thing cancer was stealing from my son, from me, and from our life together.

In the PICU there wasn't much to do. Even watching TV was boring because they only had a few stations. This was not a place to make yourself comfortable and stay awhile, not like the oncology floor where it was made for long stays. God would grab hold of me tightly during this time, pouring into me and equipping me for the battle ahead. Prayer warriors from all over the world started reaching out to me and strengthening my faith.

In the meantime, the oncologist told me how Jayden's lungs were very sick, and there wasn't anything more they could do. "He can go back up to the floor, but you will have to sign a DNR or DNI. This doesn't mean we aren't going to take good care of him. It's just policy if you want him out of the PICU."

"Would you please explain that to him?" I just couldn't have another conversation with Jayden about his death.

"Absolutely. Is there anything you don't want me to say?"

"Just be honest and answer his questions." I didn't want Jayden to think or feel like I was hiding anything from him.

Jayden was completely shattered by the news. He wasn't ready to die. He was scared for himself, but mostly worried about me. I signed a DNI, Do Not Intubate, and we were back on the floor with our family within a day or two.

There was laughter and joy again. God timed it so perfectly, while one of Jayden's best friends was visiting. They got to play some PlayStation and create a video for Instagram. I would spend the next couple of days working with the nurses and case management to get all the new equipment approved in order for us to go home. Jayden needed high flow oxygen and a BiPap machine.

If I hadn't earned my honorary nursing degree by then, I sure had now with everything I was doing. Jayden needed meds around the clock, as well as vitals checked regularly. I emptied his catheter bag and helped him with almost every task that needed to be done. Jayden struggled to do the smallest things, even talking.

We had been home for a week, and I was battling on my son's behalf. I would be up until two or three o'clock in the morning, praying in the spirit. I would anoint the house and Jayden constantly. I was desperate.

I missed going to church and missed having fellowship with my friends so I started having a Bible study every third Friday of the month. On one Friday morning, I stayed in prayer much longer than I normally do. I'd had a vision that strengthened me, and I couldn't wait to share it with my friends.

Just before the vision, I needed to see God, I needed to speak with Him. My son was in his room dying and I needed to know what God's plan was. I put on the full armor of God, praying it over myself. I clothed myself with mercy, grace, and righteousness. I placed the crown of life on my head, and all of the sudden I arrived.

I looked up to see beautiful mountains with colors so vivid it could only be a picture of heaven. I saw a green valley that went on for miles into the distance with a river flowing down the center of the valley. The sun was shining bright and there was a slight breeze. I didn't know exactly where I was going, but I knew I had to get over there, past the mountains, to get to God.

I started walking by the river, my sword in one hand and my shield in another. I was walking with a purpose, my spirit knew where we were to go. I couldn't see anything else as I walked through the valley, but I felt myself stabbing things with my sword, which was more like a dagger. I would be walking, and my arm would strike something, but my attention never moved toward the thing, I just kept focused on getting to God.

Then the scene changed from a beautiful green valley to a royal gold courtroom. I saw the 24 elders and angelic beings all around. I felt so small as I looked up to what I think was His throne. In a flash, a bright light came down and stood in front of me. He became my size, like a man's size. He hugged me. As He hugged me, He told me that He loved me. He said that He was always with me, and He would never leave me nor forsake me. I stood speechless. I soaked in every word He was saying.

He then looked to some angels standing by and told them to strengthen me. The angels started to flutter their wings as my arms opened wide and my hair blew behind me. A fresh wind. And just as quickly as I was there, I was back in my room.

When I shared this with my friends at the Bible study, I could feel the same feelings I had felt while I was with God. I could see the vision just as clearly as I had seen it that morning. We went on to talk about Jesus' first miracle, turning water into wine. We prayed over Jayden, and they departed for the night.

I felt good, I felt full, I felt hope for the first time in a while.

As the clock struck midnight, everything changed.

Jayden's oxygen plummeted, and I almost lost him right then and there in my arms. He came back, and we were able to steady his oxygen. I knew we had to go to the hospital, I wasn't going to be able to keep this up all night. I was going to worry myself sick. But Jayden wasn't able to move without losing his breath completely, and he was so swollen that he couldn't fit in his wheelchair anymore.

"I need you to mentally prepare yourself. I am going to pack our bags and call 9-1-1. You can't get to the car, and we need to get to the hospital." Jayden knew it was true, but it didn't make it hurt any less. I wonder if he knew what was happening. He mentally prepared, and I packed, praying and reminding God what He had told me and shown me.

I dialed 9-1-1, and the dispatcher asked what my emergency was. "I need a courtesy ride to Medical City Dallas Children's Hospital, please. My son is on hospice, and his oxygen is tanking, I cannot get him into the car, or I would take him." I wanted to stress the point that this was my last resort. It needed to be done, and I couldn't afford to pay for it.

Within minutes, Fire Station 8 was at my house. They were dumbfounded that I was the only one home with Jayden. They were in awe that I had been caring for him by myself this entire time. They checked him out, got him stable enough to transport, loaded him up, and we took off. I followed behind them with all our stuff because my goal was to come back home. I cried out to God the entire way.

"What are your wishes here, ma'am?" The emergency room doctor asked me. He was compassionate but had a tone of realism in his voice.

"Tune us up and send us home. If you call the charge nurse on six northwest, they will know what to do." He looked surprised that I was calling the shots. I wanted us on the floor as soon as possible because as any oncology mom knows, ER nurses aren't always equipped with what an oncology kid needs.

I consented to another DNI, and we were up on the floor. All Jayden was worried about was his lunch with Pastor Cyd, our beloved Pastor Ricky's wife. Jayden had taken it upon himself to make sure he kept in touch with her. Their bond had deepened each and every

Sunday since Pastor Ricky's passing, to the point where Jayden was now calling her Aunt Cyd.

She was scheduled to come over to our house for lunch that day, but we were in the hospital. Jayden didn't understand why I wouldn't call her to see if she could come to the hospital, but it was 4 a.m. on Saturday! Time wasn't a concern for him, but his lunch date was. We would finally settle in our room, getting Jayden all hooked up around five o'clock that morning. We both dozed off quickly.

Jayden finally texted Pastor Cyd to make lunch plans, and I consented by sleepily giving my order along with his. I was in and out for several hours but finally woke up around three in the afternoon, and we had lunch with Pastor Cyd. It was a beautiful time of laughing and storytelling.

That was Jayden's last meal and the last visitor he was fully awake to see.

Around 4 a.m. on Sunday, about 24 hours after we had gotten our room on the floor, Jayden's oxygen started to decline again. Every time this happened, Jayden would freak out and come out of the experience terrified. I was burdened watching my son suffer like this. It was pure torture.

The oncologist spoke to me as plainly as he could. "I want to paint a very clear picture here. Jayden will not be going home. He is dying." Tears started to well up in my eyes as he was speaking, I knew it was time.

They weren't expecting him to make it past noon, but in Jayden fashion he held on. I sent out a text to some of my closest friends and prayer warriors: *Jayden is not going to be coming home with me. Please pray!*

I sent an extra text to one of my best friends: *I need something from my house. It is a heartbeat necklace, it's on my dresser. Could you get it and bring it here ASAP? I am running out of time.*

Within an hour, I had a bag full of the stuff I needed, and within another hour church was letting out. God was sending people to us. Before I knew it, the floor was full of my people, Jayden's people.

Jayden would spend the next twelve hours in and out of consciousness, saying his good-byes to everyone. It was precious watching Jayden use what little breath he had left to love on everyone one last time. I kicked everyone out every few hours to have some alone time with Jayden and cry at the foot of his bed.

"M-mm-mmore m-mm-med-ii-cine." Jayden would mumble as everyone in the room sucked in a breath to hear what he had to say. I called in the nurse and called it a night for everyone who was still there. It was almost midnight.

"Are you done fighting?" I asked him as I stroked his hair, a tear falling down my cheek.

He nodded and faintly said, "I'm done fighting, I am ready to go to sleep. I love you, mom."

"I love you too, son. You did so good. I am so proud of you." I kissed his forehead, and they cranked up the medicine to make him more comfortable. He was still gasping for air every couple of hours, but now he was ready to be done, to be comfortable, to be at peace.

I had four friends stay with me through the night. Morgan had just gotten there from College Station. She came in the room and miraculously Jayden woke up. They exchanged some looks and a few words, then he nodded back off. My friends would each rotate coming in one at a time, comforting me and spending some time with Jayden.

My friend Neva's turn was next. She sat down, and I looked at her, "At this point in time, it is whatever God's will is." The words came out much easier than I wanted them to, but then they came out again. "Whatever God's will is, let it be done."

And a second later Jayden took his last breath.

I'd been expecting this moment all day, but it was still too soon.

"That's it? He's gone?" I asked the nurse. I was shocked by what I had just seen and heard.

That was my son's final breath.

The nurse gave me a quick nod and went over to take the mask off of his face and turn the machine off.

I fell into Jayden's arms, crying on his shoulder.

All I could say was, "Come back ... Please, come back ..."

PART TWO

MY SECOND LIFETIME

*The Lord is near to the brokenhearted
and saves the crushed in spirit.*

Psalm 34:18 ESV

CHAPTER 16

LIFE IS BUT A VAPOR

How do you know what your life will be like tomorrow? Your life is like the morning fog– it's here a little while, then it's gone.

James 4:14 NLT

● ● ● ● ● ● ● ● ● ● ● ● ● ● ●

A FEW HOURS after Jayden's last breath, I called my spiritual mother. I needed her guidance and comfort. She had been walking me through my grief during this entire cancer journey.

"I'm on my way sweetie." She was at the hospital within an hour.

Then I called Kammie. I needed her too; she had been through this with other families.

"I know, I know. I am sorry. I'll be up there soon." When she came, her hug was just what I needed.

My mom was next. "Mom, I need you. He's gone. I don't know what to do. I need your help." She knew how to take care of things logistically. She would be able to make arrangements with the funeral home because I was stuck. I just wanted to stay in my son's arms.

It was 4:12 a.m. when my son took his last breath. I held him for eight hours, crying, sobbing, wailing the entire time. The skin underneath my eyes was raw from wiping so many tears away. Every time I looked up at him and saw his face with no life in it, my heartbreak restarted. People were in and out all day long, I can't tell you who was there, but I have a pretty good idea. I would have held him longer, but it was time for him to be bathed. The nurses came in with a bowl of soapy water, washcloths, and a fresh blanket.

My eyes dried up as I bathed my beloved son, sharing in a few laughs with the nurses. We had so many memories with them, funny memories only we could understand. They warned me not to freak out if I saw any weird discoloration; it was normal for the blood to pool in specific areas. His skin tone was dusty, his lips were cracking, he was frozen in time.

Jayden didn't look like himself at all.

I had no idea there were rules when a child dies. One of them is that no other visitors are allowed to see the body after it is bathed. I told the nurses and doctors they were allowed in while we waited for the funeral home. The news made its way around the hospital and many hospital staff came by to give their condolences. Jayden was well loved.

"He looks so peaceful," many people said. I had a hard time seeing it at first, but these people had seen death more often than I had. They knew what they were talking about. I let that be something I held onto.

My son was now in the arms of the Prince of Peace Himself. Thinking about their reunion and how Jayden was now pain free and cancer free, I was able to see the peacefulness and smile.

I had one more moment alone with my son. I bent over to kiss his lips. They were dry and stiff.

"I guess my race here isn't done yet. I will see you when it is. I love you so much, son." I touched his hair and smelled him one last time.

Then people from the funeral home came into the room and moved him to their gurney.

"Take good care of my boy!" I said to the young lady as if Jayden were still living and breathing.

"I will, don't worry. He is in good hands."

I walked out of the doors on the oncology floor, following my son and security. It was a surprise that I wasn't allowed to get on the same elevator as Jayden's gurney, another rule. This was the end of the road. The elevator door closed, my second-to-last goodbye to my precious boy.

The lobby was full of concerned friends and family. They had been waiting at least an hour. All I wanted to do was go home, take a shower, and be alone. I had shared the last thirty-six hours with many people, and I needed to be alone. It took some repeating but everyone respected my wishes.

I couldn't comprehend what had just happened. I was completely numb.

My friends who had stayed overnight in the hospital with me went to my house before I got there to clean up and clean out. I had enough drugs in my house to overdose a hundred times over. We had left in such a hurry that Jayden's medical equipment was spread across his room— tubes, wires, and machines. The nurses instructed them to get rid of all the medication and to get all the equipment out of sight.

They did a good job of throwing all the medical equipment into Jayden's closet, but medication was everywhere. I wasn't suicidal;

I never had been. I was just dead inside, completely numb. When I finally got to be alone, I showered. I closed my eyes, wishing the water would wash away this nightmare. As I opened my eyes, my sight was blurry with tears, and the mourning started all over again. This time I let myself freely scream, cry, wail, yell, whisper, and express my emotions. Whatever came to me, came out of me. It was just me and God, and I let it all out. As I did, I remembered Jayden saying those exact words to me.

After his doctor had told him he wasn't going home with me, that he was dying, Jayden looked to me. He could see the sadness and fear in my eyes. He called me over to his bedside for a hug. As I wrapped my arms around my son, he was barely able to speak, but he said, "It's okay, mom. Let it all out."

He never liked seeing me sad. To see me cry hurt him more than it hurt me. But I did … I let it all out. For the next few weeks, the sadness was something I had never experienced before. If it weren't for Chico, I don't know if I would have gotten out of bed the following days or weeks.

I found myself in Jayden's room all the time, forcing my mind to feel the emptiness to know that it was real. I laid in his bed, wrapped in his blankets, holding his pillows close, smelling the scent that lingered. I wore his hoodies and felt as if he were hugging me. I would start to text him and realize he was gone. I would go to clean his bathroom and realize it was already clean because it had been unused.

I still had my morning prayer time with God each day. We weren't really on speaking terms, but I kept showing up. I needed Him to show me His Word is true. That He did love me and had a good plan for me. I wanted to be like Job and bless the name of the Lord who both gives and takes away.

Everything had changed with his one, last breath.

I chose the date of Jayden's celebration of life to be February 2nd. He would have liked that it was two twos and during black history month. There were many decisions that had to be made for Jayden's celebration and that gave me something to do for Jayden. I picked out the flowers and the casket. My church put together a program that was designed like a sports magazine. It would have been "Jayden approved." I ordered a dress, made memory boards, and invited anyone and everyone who wanted to come.

The day started out beautifully. My friends came over to get ready with me. I had gotten my makeup done and was ready to see my son's body for the last time. My goal for the day was to have joy and to celebrate Jayden. I could be sad later, at home, by myself, like I had been the past eleven days.

When I arrived at the church, I went straight to my boy. I wanted to make sure he looked good. I had picked out a black long sleeve button up shirt with a yellow tie and a yellow cancer ribbon pin. I had also instructed the funeral home about Jayden's hair. I wanted them to edge up his sides but to keep the length. Jayden's hair had always been a big deal, but it was an even bigger deal after cancer and losing it multiple times. They did a good job.

My son didn't look like my son, though. My Jayden was no longer in that body, and I could see it. He didn't look like he was sleeping. He looked dead, like there was no life anywhere. I didn't spend too much time with him; that was not how I wanted to remember him. I touched his hair, his beautiful afro that he had been taking such good care of. It was soft and felt the same as always. Nothing else did. Everything else was cold and stiff.

When the doors opened for the viewing to start, I stood next to the casket, hugging everyone as they came to say their final goodbye. I smiled and felt the love in the room. People from each stage of

Jayden's life had come. It was like memories playing over in my head as I hugged people I hadn't seen in years. My heart swelled, and the room started to fill. My son had impacted all of these lives. As the thought came to mind, I flashed back to Pastor Ricky's funeral. Back then, I had seen the moment I was living now. As much as I had rejected it, God had been preparing me.

What Paul says about God's grace is true: It is sufficient, it is enough.

Jayden's godfather spoke first, then Jayden's first youth pastor, then Kammie, then Pastor Cyd, then me. Everyone held their breath as I walked to the stage. I wanted to thank everyone. I wanted to thank them for their support and prayers over the past five years. I wanted to thank them for being there. I wanted to express my gratitude the only way I knew how—to say it and mean it.

We had a police escort to the gravesite where a few more kind words were shared before they planted my son into the ground. The funeral home wasn't able to get people to leave in the time that was allotted for us. Jayden's best friends were the last ones at his grave. All of them were experiencing their first death of a close friend. My heart broke for them, too. Then we all shared a meal together and said our goodbyes.

I went home by myself to be alone with my grief and my God.

CHAPTER 17

WHO AM I?

*I am feeble and severely broken; I groan
because of the turmoil of my heart.*

Psalm 38:8 ESV

• • • • • • • • • • • • • • • •

I KNEW I couldn't not work; I had bills to pay. My job offered for me
to come back, which was great news. I was just not ready, yet.

"How much time do you think you'll need?"

"I am going to take a month to just be. I have no idea who I am." I
started to feel the lump in my throat emerge and kept the conversation
short. For someone who didn't cry a lot before losing a child, I could
now cry at the simple thought of my son. Tears fell freely from my
eyes at random and unwanted times. I wondered, *Is this going to go on
forever? Will I cry every day for the rest of my life?*

I needed time in the unfamiliar territory of being single with no
children.

I had never lived one adult day without my son. I had no idea
what it was like to not work full time, go to school full time, be a
single mom full time, and take care of my household full time. It was
all I had known. Now I felt as if I had all the time in the world and

needed to fill it. But first, healing. I didn't want any lingering trauma to go unaddressed.

It was time to get back to work ... on the inside.

Ashley's Grief Journal

February 9, 2024

It's been one week since Jayden's Celebration. My heart aches a little more each day. With each day that goes by, the reality of that day sinks in a little deeper. When I close my eyes I can see you taking your last breath. I can remember the last couple of moments, the last couple of days, the last couple of weeks. I could sit all day thinking about it. My heart longs for a redo, a do over! If I had only known.

I try not to think about Jayden for a long period of time. It just makes me cry and feel sad. I want so badly to know what I want to do and where I want to work. I want a timeline. I want a checklist. There isn't one. I am just to bare this pain each morning and try to build myself up throughout the day. I still sit with God, but it is different. I go through the motions and I hear from Him from time to time, but it is not the same coffee dates we used to have. A part of me is gone, and a huge part of my prayer life is gone.

I was pregnant at such a young age, but from that moment on, I was his mom. I have never pictured a day of my life without him. Without him being a text or a phone call away. Without him being in the other room. Without him next to me. This is not what I wanted.

This hurts so bad, but I am going to choose to trust God and be confident in His Word that He will work this out for my good and His purpose. I will see Jayden again real soon. I hope to see him in my everyday life here on earth, too.

February 11, 2024

It is Sunday! I think my body, soul, and spirit all knew it, too. I woke up and for a slight moment I second-guessed going to church in person. Then I felt the excitement of going to church jolt through my body. As I went about getting ready I would be sad for a moment and then the joy of going to the House of the Lord would take over. It was an easier morning because I knew I would be in the presence of the Lord.

I was two minutes late; who am I? I am never late. Being late makes me stress out. But not now, not today. Each step I took required a deep breath. Every time I looked up, I tried to not see anyone I knew. I found a seat in the middle amongst the crowd, far enough back, far enough in the row. I worshiped. I took notes. Prayed. Praised.

I sat and debated for a good five minutes with myself if I was going to hurry up and leave or go slowly and say hi to people. Before I knew it, church was letting out, and I had not come up with a plan yet. I just started walking in pace with the crowd. I was booking it to my car, and right in front of me was Alexis Martin. She hugged me and said, "Everyone was texting me that you were here."

I knew it, there was no way to sneak in or sneak out of this place. It was home, it has been home for almost ten years. I saw a few more people, and as I was traveling through the church building, I felt something missing. A big part of me was missing.

Jayden loved going to church. All his best friends were there. We spent at least two days a week there, and I had been working there for the past three years. Church, especially this church, holds so many memories. I thought if I were to ever lose Jayden, I would want to run as far away as possible. But it turns out I want to be close to all my memories with him. It is hard, but it also brings me joy. Everyone knew Jayden. Jayden made himself known. He was loved very much by his church family.

Of course when I got home I lost it. My heart broke all over again. It's just me. It's no longer Ashley and Jayden, just Ashley. Ashley is learning how to navigate life as just Ashley. God is slowly showing me. He is giving me new perspectives, new ideas, new journeys, and most of all loving me through it all.

God has given me a book idea and has asked me to write like crazy this week. Church was all about obedience today. I choose level four, daily obedience!

February 14, 2024

Happy Valentine's Day! My first one without you. I'm going to see what they have at Target and bring you something. I know on this day you would have made me feel extra loved. You always wanted me to have a husband, but I just had no luck.

Really, you were enough for me. I even once told God I would give up the desire for a husband if He healed you on this side of eternity. I pictured you with a big purple heart balloon for me this morning. I loved it!

I took Chico to the vet yesterday, and he's lost 1.4 pounds! I know! I really wanted to text you and tell you. I try to think of what your response would be, and I think it would be the mind blown emoji or maybe even disbelief.

I woke up at 4 a.m. again with you on my mind. I tried to go back to sleep three times, but kept waking up with a different thought. I've rethought my plan for your room. Chico loves being in there with the window open and sun on him! I also love sitting on your bed and reading or writing. There's plenty of room for me to clean it out and put a treadmill in there because that's really all I need to make my home gym complete! Morgan and Payton are also coming next weekend to stay, and I'll be staying in your room. I like the idea of having a spare bed for someone. I like the idea of not changing your room too much, but maybe repurposing the space.

I can see myself working at the desk in the hall. You know, opening all my non-profits and consulting with people. Running each morning, facing the sunrise and our favorite tree! I love writing in your room. I feel a new level of encouragement here from you. I'll keep the TV and your computer, but I am going to get rid of these gaming systems.

I am doing better. I'm not crying all the time, but I do still allow myself space to cry. I can feel myself missing you throughout the day. My routine has really helped me. It's given me steps to take and goals to reach. You know how I love that! I've tried to talk myself out of a lot of things, but I just keep going! Jayden is my motivation! Jayden is my why! I think about your strength and courage, son, and I just keep going! Thank you for that!

I love you and miss you more each day! Have fun celebrating love with our Father!

February 18, 2024

Plans at the lake house didn't totally go according to plan, but that is okay! I was going to stay tonight as well but found out last night that everyone was leaving tonight so Chico and I are home. Missing you, son! A wave of emotions hit me like I have never experienced before. Life without you is becoming so real, and I don't like it one bit!

First of all, not having you at the lake house was hard. I felt your absence. After I was able to get it together to pack for this weekend trip, I cried most of the drive there. It was the 17th, my first time packing since I called 911, and my first time driving a road trip without my boy. My emotions were flowing. I also saw you on my drive. Any time I saw our favorite fast food places. Or a cross.

O, how I miss you, son.

As soon as I got to the lake, Ruby invited me (and everyone) to a fancy dinner party. We went shopping and then came home to get ready. I made Ramen and Asian apps, BooBoo got pizza.

We had conversation starters and everything! I know you would have enjoyed it. I felt like something was missing from me, and there was ... you!

As I was driving home, getting closer and closer to the house, I almost felt an excitement like I was coming home to you or that you were with me and we were almost home. Painfully, I realized neither were true. You are with Jesus, and I am here. O God, this is hard. Please help me through this pain!

February 22, 2024

One month. You've been with Jesus for one month. I have learned so much in one month. You, your life, has taught me so much, son, thank you! I thank God for picking me to be your mom, even though my time with you was short. I almost feel as if our time together was a full lifetime. For you, it was. You loved me and everyone around you so well, I can see and feel you everywhere!

When the sun is shining bright in the sky, I think about the song, You are my Sunshine. You are my Sonshine! When I see yellow flowers or hear the birds singing or see anything TCU, I think about you and feel you are near. I say good morning to you every morning when I open your curtains and good night each night when I close them. I spend time in your room reading, writing, or watching sermons. I can feel you!

I get excited when I think about the things God has put on my heart to start in honor of you and your life.

I saw the Darby's today at women's Bible study, and man, do

I love them. They are family! Everyone is still working through some emotions and questions, but we are working on them. No one is standing still. We all want to honor you well. Many times over, I have had someone tell me you helped get them through something. I know for me you are my why in a whole new way!

As sad and as tragic as all this is for us, I see now that I can do all things through Christ who strengthens me. I am ready to continue running my race and beat my mile! Love is all that matters! Faith, hope, and love. The greatest of these is love. I love you, son, and I am going to finish this thing strong for us! God is for me! God is with me! God is good!

My life is all about honoring Jayden now. I want to find myself, do big things, and make a lasting impact ...

... all for Jayden Xavior Simmons!

CHAPTER 18

RESUMING LIFE

The Lord Himself goes before you and will be with you;
He will never leave you nor forsake you. Do not be afraid;
do not be discouraged.

Deuteronomy 31:8 NIV

* * * * * * * * * * * * * * *

"I'M GOING TO have an *Eat, Pray, Love* year!" I said, letting my family and friends in on my plans for what was going to be the hardest year of my life. First up was Colorado for spring break.

It was supposed to be an annual trip Jayden and I took with our friends who had become family. I contemplated whether or not to go and felt like it might be good to get away. Jayden loved snow. Maybe I would enjoy it for him this year. I thought about getting out in the mountains and soaking in the Glenwood Springs, convincing myself this would be refreshing for my soul.

It was the start of my adventures. I would travel, see the world, find Jayden in it all, and do things I never had the chance to do because I was a young single mom all my adult life. Traveling the world to find myself would happen just like it does in the movies.

The first night of our stay, a wild snow storm went through Denver, and we received forty inches of snow. Waking up the next morning to have coffee and seeing the ground covered in a down comforter of white snow, I smiled with little tears in my eyes. As I stared out the window, I felt Jayden's presence so near. I snowshoed in those forty inches, and it was hard work! I dipped in the healing waters of Glenwood Springs and explored the cute little mountain towns, hitting up a couple oxygen bars along the way.

Six days and five nights was a bit much for me. I got homesick. I needed space in order to let it all out, and I didn't really have that in a house of ten people. I knew none of them would judge me if I started to cry—heck, I'm sure they'd cry too, we were all mourning Jayden—but I wasn't able to let myself fully mourn when I was around other people. It was sacred; it was private.

After my trip, I resumed going back to work. My position adjusted a little bit, and was more up my alley, writing curriculum and creating resources for various ministries. I loved seeing all my coworkers and being around people again. I have been an extrovert my whole life. People give me energy most of the time. I had my slow mornings and my hard days. I accepted them, sat in them, went in late if I needed to. Grief sometimes stayed in my heart, while other times it came rushing out of me like white water rapids.

Remembering Jayden, every detail of him, became an obsession. I thought I was going to forget him. When that fear started to consume me, I decided to reach out to another mom I had met during Jayden's treatment who had lost her son three years prior.

"Can you still see and remember him exactly how he was? I woke up this morning, wondering if I would forget. It made me sad, so I thought I'd ask."

"Yes! I can see his face as clear as if I'd seen him yesterday. I can still hear his voice, and I remember many of the things he said in his own quirky way. We speak of him regularly and share our memories. I remember the fear you're describing. When it plagued me, I copied all the photos and videos of him into a folder of just him so that it would always be easy to find. Later, I composed a book of many of my memories of him. Since then, I've realized that he's a large part of me. I won't forget. The same is true for you. Jayden is a part of you. Nothing will change that. In raising him, he taught you a million things. Being his mom helped shape you into the wonderful woman you are today. You won't lose that. I'm sorry you woke up in fear. Hug."

That she was experiencing similar feelings made me feel normal. It was then I realized I needed to join a grief group. I needed people who I could relate to who had been doing this longer than me. The picture I had in my mind for a grief group was similar to what I saw in movies of an AA meeting. People would talk, address their feelings, state where they were at and heal. I didn't want a group where we watched video clips or were given a workbook or with someone who had lost their great-grandma. (Great-grandmas matter, but it is not the same as losing my one and only son.)

I searched the internet and found one organization for families who have lost children. I found the chapter closest to me and put the fourth Tuesday on my calendar.

As the fourth Tuesday of the month approached, I felt the heaviness of what I was about to step into. I was unable to focus, I just kept thinking about what it was going to be like. My mind was on a hamster wheel of what ifs and possible scenarios. I was determined to go.

I went. As soon as I stepped into the room, a spirit of heaviness fell on me. There were already people sitting down, tissues in their hands ready to go. Everyone was practically silent. I just kept taking deep breaths.

The leader for the night started off by giving us the agenda for the group sessions. First we celebrated birthdays. Parents whose child's birthday was in March had the opportunity to bring their child's favorite treat and share a favorite memory with everyone. I noticed there was a board with all the children's pictures on it so I made a mental note to bring a picture next time. We then were to pass around a stone with the word "courage" engraved on it. When you had the stone, it was your turn to share. They asked us to share what we wanted to, giving us a little direction: our name, our child's name, how they died, when they died, and where we are on our journey. Once everyone who wanted to share had shared, then we would have a topic with a small teaching and an open discussion.

I sat and listened to a woman share about her son for his birthday, but don't remember much about what she said, I was silently planning Jayden's celebration in my head. When the stone was passed around, the stories started to invoke all sorts of emotions inside of me. Tears were on the verge of falling, my palms were sweating, and my heart was racing as I saw the stone coming closer to me. I heard stories of suicide, of drug overdoseing, of murder, of accidents, and of some unexplainable deaths. My heart broke for everyone in the room, and I'm sure the feeling was mutual.

The stone was in my hand, and it was my turn ... courage. I held the stone and closed my eyes, taking a deep breath. I tried to open my mouth to say my name, but my lips just quivered. The tears started to roll down my face. The ugly cry was about to happen. I looked down at the rock and mustered up the courage.

"My name is Ashley," was all I could get out before I started to cry. I felt a hand touch me. My neighbor knew exactly where I was. She later apologized for touching me, but it was just what I needed to keep going.

"My son's name is Jayden, and he passed away two months ago, January 22, from osteosarcoma—bone cancer. I'm having a really hard time. I had Jayden when I was in high school so I don't know what it is like to be just me. Please tell me this gets better?" I sobbed the entire time I talked. I then passed the stone to my neighbor. She lost her 16-year-old daughter in an accident. We connected right away. I continued going to grief group, continued processing, continued trying to keep saying yes to life.

For Valentine's Day I bought a kit to make Valentine's hearts for Jayden. I collected some small stones to place the doily hearts over the still fresh dirt of Jayden's grave. For Easter, I invited family and friends over to make Jayden Easter eggs. Then we took a trip to his grave and placed them for him to find. As school was ending in May, I invited people over to paint summer stones for Jayden.

This is how I coped. I felt like I was doing something for Jayden. Bringing people together helped us all heal in a way that being apart couldn't. We were all carrying Jayden in our hearts, trying to find somewhere for all our love to go. The attention to detail teenage boys put into these crafts was remarkable. Everyone wanted to honor Jayden.

As the hours, days, weeks, and months started to go by, I realized I was doing it. I was living. I was able to do things like work, hang out with friends, go on trips, laugh, and be thankful.

Also, I was learning how to live with my new friend grief. We had a very rocky relationship.

I would continually replay God's Words from my visit to the Throne Room:

I love you, Ashley. I am with you. I will never leave you nor forsake you.

A broken record of truth.

CHAPTER 19

IS THIS SOME KIND
OF SICK JOKE?

*How long must I struggle with anguish in my soul, with
sorrow in my heart every day? How long will my enemy
have the upper hand?*

Psalm 13:2 NLT

• • • • • • • • • • •• • • •

MOM TEXTED THE siblings group chat: *In the emergency room
with your dad. Something is not right.*

> **Me:** *What's going on?*
> **Mom:** *His breathing is bad, fatigue, no appetite, weakness in legs,
> I had to help him get dressed.*
> **Me:** *Where are you?*

I was already packing to make the 2-hour drive and be there
for my parents. They were in Quitman or "the big city" as my dad

called it. Yantis, where they had a tiny home in a small retirement community, was "tiny town" to him.

I finally made it to Quitman and started to experience the worst deja vu imaginable. I walked into my dad's room to see him on oxygen with labored breathing.

"His belly looks distended, how much fluid is he getting?" I asked the nurse as she came in to greet me.

"Are you in the medical field?"

"Yeah, this is my 'doctor daughter,'" My dad quipped.

"No, I am just knowledgeable," I said, smiling. Within minutes, the doctor was in the room to explain what was going on. My dad had pneumonia and was about to be CareFlighted to the ICU unit in Tyler. That doctor also noticed my questions and asked if I were a doctor, and again, I had to let him know I wasn't.

I went out to the waiting room to tell my mom the plan, and I hit the road. Tyler was about an hour away. I wanted to get there as soon as possible. My dad was going to be there in five minutes. I needed to make sure he was getting the best care.

Because my brother and my mom stayed in Quitman until my dad took off, I was the first to arrive in Tyler. I found my way to the ICU, where my dad was still on oxygen and struggling. I knew he had been battling bladder cancer for a couple of years, but everything seemed to be going well with treatment. I also knew he had Chronic Obstructive Pulmonary Disease, or COPD, but I had no idea how sick he really was.

He had a two-inch tumor in his lungs, close to his windpipe.

All I could think was, Jesus, please. Not my dad too.

That year, my family had taken two losses already—Jayden and my sister-in-law's cousin—Madeline, whom we all knew and loved. She was barely an adult when she started experiencing complications with an autoimmune disorder she had been living with for years. One of my good friends also lost her mom exactly a month after Jayden passed. She'd had COPD and pneumonia. The year 2024 was turning out to be the year my family was stretched beyond what we ever thought imaginable. It wasn't even April, yet.

They were asking the standard questions, and since this was a teaching hospital, it happened several times. The plan was to start him on antibiotics, monitor the pneumonia, and start him on a BiPap machine. My heart sank, knowing that my son had died on a BiPap machine. My faith was shaky, all I could see was death. I started to feel the lies engulf me again.

The staff at this hospital also asked if I was in the medical field, and every time, my dad told them that I was his "doctor daughter." Being a daddy's girl, I knew how proud my dad was of me.

I reported all the news to my family and made the call to tell my dad's sister. She lived in Indiana and would need to fly in soon. My mom wanted her to wait a day or two to see if there was any improvement. They had just been here less than two months before for Jayden's funeral. I could understand wanting to wait, but I also saw that my dad's lungs were very sick.

The words of Jayden's oncologist replayed in my head, "There's not much we can do when the lungs get sick."

I felt the sooner she made it down here, the more time she would have with him while he was awake. I knew how situations like this could spiral downhill quickly.

I discovered the rules for adult patients were quite different than for children. I went to every scan and every treatment room. I stayed the night and moved in with my son when he was in the hospital. That was not the case with my dad. Visiting hours were from 10 a.m.-

2 p.m. and 4 p.m.-10 p.m. They gave my mom some grace, but the rest of us had to go.

I noticed some cops were with the patient next door to my dad. Leaning into my brother's ear, I smirked, "I'll leave when those cops decide to leave."

He had noticed them too. We figured a fellow police officer must have been in some sort of accident.

The nurse noticed we were hanging out longer than we were supposed to. She approached us and in a very gentle voice told us visiting hours were over. I, thinking I knew better, asked why the cops got to stay. To my surprise the patient in the bed next door to my dad was an inmate at the local county jail. We said our goodbyes and headed to our hotel room.

I knew my mom was scared so I stayed close by in East Texas over the weekend—Easter weekend. When reports kept coming back with news that the pneumonia was not responding to antibiotics and that there were other complications due to COPD and the tumor, my dad was now on high-flow oxygen all day and a BiPap all night. This was exactly what happened to Jayden.

My heart broke for my family, knowing what was about to happen. I stayed in East Texas another week. During that time, we viewed the total solar eclipse, which was beautiful out in the wide open country. It reminded me God was in control. I tried to pray, I tried to muster up the courage to talk with my dad about Jesus, but I was stuck. I felt frozen in time. My heart and my head could not process what was happening.

Soon my dad was on a ventilator. His body needed to rest while medicine tried to dissolve the infections in his blood and lungs.

Eventually, I had to drive back home. One night there was a text alert on my phone. I looked and saw it was from my mom. Things progressed quickly from there.

2:52 a.m: *I'm back in the hospital. They called at 1:00, and he had coded, but they resuscitated him. He is still with us but it doesn't look good at this time.*

7:21 a.m.: *I have asked for your dad to be taken off the vent. This is a battle he will unfortunately not be able to overcome. Please remember him for the dad he was and how much he loved you all.*

8:22 a.m.: *Your dad passed away. He is at peace now.*

Ten minutes before that last text came through, I had packed and gotten into my car. I knew my mom would need someone to be there with her for at least a little bit. I couldn't cry for my dad without thinking about Jayden. I wanted so badly to grieve my dad and only my dad, but my mind wouldn't let me. I flashed back to a phone call I'd had with my dad after Jayden had passed.

"I was dreaming I had gotten up to go to the bathroom. My back started to itch so I grabbed a spatula from the drawer and started to scratch it." As my dad explained his dream to me, I smiled because it sounded like something that would happen in real life. "When I turned around, there were a bunch of white feathers everywhere. I thought to myself, I'll clean this up in the morning. When morning came, there were no feathers. I woke up from the dream, and it was 2:03 a.m.. When you posted that Jayden grew his angel wings, it made me think about the feathers."

"Wow dad! Thanks for sharing. I wonder what it could mean? Maybe Jayden was coming to visit you since you weren't able to say goodbye to him."

"Maybe," my dad said, choking up a bit. "I love you, baby. You doing okay?"

"I'm doing the best I can, I think."

At the time, the dream seemed to be about Jayden. In retrospect, that dream meant many things I never thought about when I first heard it. I knew my dad had also grown a pair of angel wings. Jayden was at heaven's gates, waiting for him, arms stretched wide. Jayden was praying from heaven while we were praying from earth. My dad was safe in our Heavenly Father's arms, walking the streets of gold with my one and only son. My faith and the faith of my family were enough.

We had a beautiful celebration of life for my dad. He was a simple man who wasn't religious but loved his family and his community. When planning it, we wanted to honor my dad in a way that suited him. The family spent time with him at the graveside, and then we had a meal with his neighbors from their local community.

At Jayden's funeral, my dad had mentioned to my mom how much he liked Jayden's casket. Naturally, we ordered him the same one. My mom also ordered various Pittsburgh Steelers stickers, and while at the graveside, we decorated his casket with stickers he would have loved and appreciated. I gathered up songs my dad loved from everyone to make a playlist, and it was playing in the background, almost like my dad was there. We also made memory boards.

It's like we had done this before, or something.

Losing two of the most important men in my life within two months of each other brought me to a place with God I never thought I would find myself. I wrestled with Him about scriptures like John 16:33.

Why God? How is this going to work out for my good? Now my dad will never walk me down the aisle.

In this world you will have trouble.

You got that right.

But take heart.

I am trying!

I have overcome the world.

I know You have; that's why this hurts so bad. You could have prevented all of this, stopped it at any moment ...

... but You didn't.

CHAPTER 20

HOW DO I CONTINUE TO GO ON LIKE THIS?

If it is true that You look favorably on me, let me know Your ways so I may understand You more fully and continue to enjoy Your favor. And remember that this nation is Your very own people.

Exodus 33:13 NLT

● ● ● ● ● ● ● ● ● ● ● ● ● ●

"GOD AND I are now on speaking terms," I said, answering my concerned family and friends. "You know when one of your good friends says something or does something that just hurts your feelings? You know how it takes you a minute to bounce back and be able to bring it up to them?" They would nod with understanding as I continued to explain. "That's how I felt with God. I felt like He hurt me and I needed a minute to collect myself in order to be able to really express my feelings to Him. To be able to trust Him again."

I was trying to navigate a life I had never known, never dreamed of. It was all new to me. Some things were still the same, but they were also different now. The sun still rose every morning, but my days felt unfamiliar. I still worked and attended church in the same building, but I drove to and from church alone. It was harder, something was missing. My friends were still the same, but I knew I wasn't. Would they like the new me?

I continued to show up to meet with God every morning. He had the answers, and I had plenty of questions. I was able to talk more as we continued to have our coffee dates, and He continued to comfort me with His Word. I started processing my grief with God, and I began to hear Him speak.

Grief is a funny-strange-we-don't-know-what-to-do-with-it kind of thing. I was experiencing emotions I had never encountered before. The strangest one of them all was feeling two opposite emotions at the same time. I was happy for my friends' kids who were ending their school year and starting their summer but also devastated that Jayden wasn't doing the same thing. My time with God was spent treating these feelings so I could get out of my head and into His hands.

I am calling you to holiness, Ashley, He told me.

At the lowest point of my life, God was calling me to a higher place. I wanted this for me, too. I started looking at my life through a completely different lens. What mattered before just didn't matter now. What I thought was important back then just wasn't that important now. I wanted to work on my heart. If I was going to do the work of grieving, I might as well work on my heart at the same time.

Serve My people and give generously.

I was empty, and God was asking me to give. I listened and waited for opportunities to do so. It started with giving thanks to everyone who had been there for me. I could barely make it through a church service in one piece. I knew I still had some healing to do before I could pour into others. But soon enough, doing things for others helped me not to focus on me; it gave me purpose.

Be zealous for Me and My Kingdom.

I knew God was speaking to encourage me. He was speaking into my future, into days that weren't wrapped up in sadness and grief. He was calling me. He didn't want me to forget that He has good plans for my life. He wanted me to know that He delighted in me and wanted me to delight in Him, too. God never stopped pursuing me. He was close to me, near to my broken heart.

After my dad passed, I resumed the adventures I had planned. The goal was to travel, see the world, experience different cultures, eat lots of local food, pray every day, make memories, and love the life God has blessed me with.

The island of Puerto Rico was the next trip I planned after my spring break in Colorado. This time it was a girls trip with my three very best friends. Our house was on the beach next to an oceanside gym. We all needed this trip and were beyond grateful for my brother and sister-in-law for gifting it to us. There is just something about a beach that gives me peace and comfort like nowhere else. Most of the time when I am imagining myself talking to Jesus, He and I are on a beach somewhere.

Our only plans were to hike the El Yunque National Forest, shop in Old San Juan, and eat where the locals suggested. Hiking the rainforest was epic. It is the only tropical forest in the United States. The plant life was luscious, and the terrain was exciting. The climax of the hike was a waterfall slide and a rope swing into a natural pool that dumped into a rushing river that gets 120 inches of rain each year.

One of my friends was pregnant and not participating in the slide or the swing. I didn't want to either so we watched together. While I was watching, I gazed up at the rope swing and was struck by a beautiful Puerto Rican man. He had a backpack and was clearly a tour guide. For a second, I thought we locked eyes, but we both had sunglasses on so I wasn't sure.

Later, our group was getting ready to go into the forest and back to our tour van. We were taking one last group picture, and I noticed the beautiful man walking toward the river.

"Oh, let me help you!" I said, flirting with him a little as he approached the edge. I locked my arm in with his, and we walked across the water together.

"Thank you. You saved me." He replied, smiling. My friends' mouths were wide open in shock that I just went for it. We made it safely to land, and he headed towards his group, and I headed towards mine.

"Umm ... who is that man?" I asked our tour guide. The man and our tour guide both had yellow backpacks so I drew the conclusion that they might work together. I was right, they did.

Both groups began walking, and I took the opportunity to chat with him a little bit more. He was charming, and he enjoyed the attention from this very excited tourist ... or at least I hoped he did. Again our groups went our separate ways. My group happened to be all girls so we planned a night on the town together. We all secretly hoped the beautiful man was going to be there.

"He's the boss; he doesn't come out with us." Our tour guide let us down gently.

The next morning we experienced a blackout, and that meant no coffee. We needed coffee. There was a coffee shop up the road so we headed to get some "fuel." It was the best coffee I had ever had, and was made with homemade cashew milk. We were all sitting down enjoying our coffee when we saw a tour van pull into the gas station next door.

Out of the van popped the beautiful man! We are all shocked and trying to figure out what to do. First, we decided to stare, maybe he would feel us all looking at him. It didn't work.

Then one of my friends encouraged me to take advantage of the opportunity at hand. "Go, Ashley! It's your chance!"

"I can't go over there; I am in my pajamas!" I said, annoyed that I hadn't taken five seconds to change before we left to get the coffee.

"It's a small island, ladies. Always stay ready!" One of my friends chirped. She was wearing an ocean blue tennis dress, with her hair in a side braid. She'd been to the island many times.

And I never saw the beautiful man again. It was a lesson learned and a great memory made. Most of all, it just felt good to be enjoying life again. Slowly but surely, I was noticing that my heart was no longer numb.

We spent the rest of our time on the beach, enjoying beach activities. We swam with sea turtles and took beach runs. We had fun shopping and exploring the city of Old San Juan, trying to hit all the sightseeing moments we could. And we ate! We made sure to try mofongo everywhere we went and split a whole red fish at one point.

Puerto Rico has a special place in my heart. I felt joy and life in myself again. My friends didn't treat me differently or ignore the fact that I was grieving. They were just there, whether it was for laughing or crying, dancing or sleeping.

My next trip was a bold one. I hopped on a plane and flew across the ocean to Italy! My mom had been adopted, and she had done an ancestry DNA sequence and learned she was Italian. That made me want to go even more. Jayden and my dad's birthdays are in the same week—my dad's is the 15th of July and Jayden's is the 17th. I went in honor of them and my newly discovered culture.

I didn't know I would be taking an unintentional vow of silence, but I did. The first place I stayed was so picturesque that it could have been in the movies. The only person who spoke English was the guy at the coffee shop. It didn't stop me trying to communicate with the locals; there was just a little misunderstanding between us. Before the trip, I had practiced Italian with an app on my phone and had watched videos online. I thought I had some of the language down, but nope! They spoke way too fast and wanted to know more than just how I was doing.

The silence was torture at the time, but also healing. Because of jetlag I spent the first two days sick and sleeping every four hours. As my systems started to calm down and adjust to the time change, I started to experience Italy. I headed to Rome and the Fiumicino coast. I spent time on the beach and in the city. I loved it all!

I couldn't believe I was standing in places where people in the Bible had stood. I walked the streets Peter walked and swam the seas where Paul had shipwrecked. I felt so close to God. Experiencing Rome helped me to see the timelessness of God in a whole new way. The beauty in the architecture and in the geography of the land were breathtaking.

This trip was for me and God. He needed me out of my comfort zone, by myself and quiet so He could really minister to my heart. When I arrived back home I felt as if I could do anything. I had just gone halfway around the world by myself; there's nothing I couldn't do. With God on my side, how could I lose?

Jacksonville, North Carolina was next. I went to see a friend I had grown up with and hadn't seen for over a handful of years. She had known me before I had Jayden because we rode horses together.

She was now married with three kids of her own. We picked up right where we left off. In the car together, we started singing all the songs we used to back in the day—shout out to Shania Twain and LeeAnn Rimes— it was like no time had passed at all.

Next I went to Scottsdale, Arizona for another girls trip with my sister-in-law and her friend. She'd heard about my year of adventure and invited me to join them on a weekend getaway. Arizona is hot even in September so we spent a lot of time by the pool and in the lazy river. We laughed and made memories.

My last trip of the year was to Palo Duro Canyon—the second largest canyon in the United States. My friend whose mom passed away a month after Jayden was doing a grief run in honor of her. She was running the 50K while some of our other friends were running the 25K. I was part of the "cheer squad."

Race day was awesome! It was the only time I had ever contemplated doing anything more than a 10K race. The canyon was beautiful and the energy of honoring her mom carried all of us through the day.

I had never been able to travel like that before. I loved every second of it. God so graciously gave me the time and space, and each experience felt tailored to me. God knew exactly what I needed in order to keep moving forward, to keep living.

CHAPTER 21

FAITH, HOPE, AND LOVE

Three things will last forever– faith, hope, and love–
and the greatest of these is love.

1 Corinthians 13::13 NLT

● ● ● ● ● ● ● ● ● ● ●● ● ● ● ●

I WAS STARTING to feel like I was "behind" in my grief. I needed Jayden's phone to still be Jayden's phone, and I kept charging it. I was nowhere near wanting to turn it off. I used our text thread to send reminders to myself: links, screenshots, names, places, anything I felt like sending. It was nice to see Jayden's name pop up.

His voicemail greeting brought a smile to my face every time. In it, he was semi-mocking cell phone users from the early 2000s, where we used our stereo to play a song and then talked over it. Jayden had played a few seconds of a 50 Cent song, then his voice came sliding in, "Yo, yo, yo! It's J-dogg in this piece. If I don't answer the phone, I'm probably busy right now. Go ahead and holla at me later. Peace!"

Then the song would come back on, taking us to the tone. I loved hearing his voice.

Eventually, I texted my friend from grief group: *Did your daughter have a phone?*

Friend: *She did! I still have it and pay the monthly bill.*

Here I was thinking I was behind, like keeping his phone was wrong. What a relief that I wasn't the only one.

Me: *You never turned it off?*

Friend: *Never turned it off. I don't want anyone to have her number. I am sure I will have to when the phone becomes obsolete, but I just can't make myself do it.*

In the next grief group meeting, I shared this story and how it made me feel. I told the group how important it was for me to have people I could relate to, who could calm my irrational but very real feelings. I was surprised when almost every mother, father, family of a teenager, or young adult still had their child's phone. One mom had to upgrade her daughter's phone to keep it on the plan, and she did.

Grief group was a godsend.

Celebrating Jayden's 16th birthday in grief group was exciting for me. It was another way I felt like I was doing something for him. I ordered a chocolate chip cookie cake cut into the numbers one and six and decorated with black, white, and yellow frosting. I brought one of the memory boards I had made for his celebration of life—the sports one. I wanted my new friends to see what Jayden loved doing with his athletic abilities. I spent ten minutes talking and could have gone on and on. It was the first time in grief group I hadn't cried when talking about Jayden. Memories were starting to bring more smiles than tears as time kept going.

If there was one thing I wanted to do well, it was to honor Jayden. I didn't want his story to end. I didn't want people to forget how truly wonderful of a young man he was. Jayden had impacted many lives, and he left his mark. That thought sparked an idea for a business, Leave Your Mark Collections.

The t-shirt Jayden had designed with the Dallas Stars went so well, it inspired me to keep it going. I had a sweet sixteen shirt designed for Jayden's 16th birthday, his first birthday spent in heaven. One of Jayden's favorite verses was John 3:16, which worked perfectly for a sweet sixteen themed shirt. I had a few hats designed, as well. The mission of Leave Your Mark Collections is to honor loved ones affected by cancer to hear their story and wear their story. The vision is to eventually have many stories with many collections, sponsoring events, helping fund research, and spreading awareness.

During our fight we were very involved in several charities supporting childhood cancer families. Jayden had many little gigs here and there, and he shared his story and his smile each time. The golfball cannon was one of his favorite gigs. Charities often raise funds by having a golf ball cannon at hole eighteen during a golf tournament. For twenty bucks, a golfer can have someone shoot his first drive out of a handheld cannon rather than hit it himself. Most of the guys let Jayden shoot the cannon. His aim was much better than mine.

That was our attitude. If we were going to be forced into the world of childhood cancer, we were going to make the most of it. And if I were going to be forced into the "bereaved parent club," I would make the most of that, too.

Celebration number two of Jayden's birthday consisted of cake, tears, footballs, laughs, and a whole mess of memories shared at his graveside with family and friends. All of his people were excited to see me and wanted to make sure I was doing all right. Announcing the business and Jayden's sweet sixteen design at his graveside birthday party gave me the jolt of encouragement I needed.

My time in the hospital had been spent writing. I now had the time to finish several projects I had started years before. Self-publishing my very first devotional was new and exciting. My days of praying and soaking in God's presence while I was caregiving for my son inspired Blossoming Faith: A 90-Day Journaling Devotional for Women. I believe in our most broken state, God is able to speak to us the clearest. It's when we are at our lowest we are able to put ourselves aside and hear Him.

My life's mission started to become very clear to me. He wants me to write and to share my story. He wants me to be an advocate and voice for children who have lost their lives to the evils of cancer. He wants me to shine light on the role of caregivers and assist them by providing a safe community. He wants me to encourage and walk with other bereaved moms.

I have read it a thousand times, but when I was forced to live it, Paul's words in 1 Corinthians 13:13 took on a whole new meaning: "Three things will last forever—faith, hope, and love—and the greatest of these is love."

I knew this to be true, and experiencing it brought it to life. I am saying, "Yes God, here I am. Please, send me. I only want things that last, things that are eternal things in my life. I will share my faith, give people hope, and spread love around the world."

It wasn't all for nothing. God has a purpose for it all.

CHAPTER 22

JANUARY 2025

As the Heavens are higher than the earth, so are My ways higher than your ways and My thoughts than your thoughts.

Isaiah 55:9 NIV

● ● ● ● ● ● ● ● ● ● ●● ● ● ● ●

I DECIDED NOT to decorate for Christmas that year. It was going to be hard enough as it was. Everyone was wanting to know my plans for the holidays, and honestly, my plans were to just get through the holidays. Christmas was Jayden's favorite time of the year. He loved the cold, he loved the lights, and most of all, he loved the hot chocolate.

I couldn't bring myself to watch the movie *Elf*, go to any Christmas parties, or be in the holiday spirit. I tried my hardest to stay busy to avoid the massive emotions that come with grieving. Volunteering to be the left stage director for our Christmas production at church was a big enough task. At first everything was fine, but then we started having more rehearsals and staying later. All I could think about on those days was how Jayden loved staying at church for these kinds of things. Just walking around, being a church kid, talking to everyone, and laughing with security brought him joy. It was the little things

I missed the most, like him sitting in the front seat of the car or reminding him to pick up his towels.

That year, the production was based on Charles Dickon's *A Christmas Carol*. Watching the scenes with Tiny Tim caused me to flashback to my last Christmas with Jayden. He was too tired to go anywhere on Christmas Day. It was our first Christmas with just the three of us—Jayden, Chico, and myself. Watching Tiny Tim be healed over and over again stirred up many unwanted, unwelcomed emotions. I held myself together as I directed and let it all out when I got home. There was no escaping grief. It found me, cuddled up with me, and wanted its attention.

The weekend of the Christmas production, I started to notice some illegal activity happening with one of the maintenance men at my apartment complex. Jayden and I had lived in the same complex for almost ten years, and I had never felt unsafe until that day. I reported what I had witnessed and caught on camera to both the apartment manager as well as the corporate office. To my surprise nothing was done, and the man continued to work on property.

Suddenly I realized that I had to move. An ocean of emotion poured out of me. There was fear of leaving all my memories behind. There was hesitancy to change because I wasn't ready. There was anger because this man was getting away with crimes. I felt defeated. Vulnerable. Fragile.

If my first Christmas without Jayden wasn't hard enough, now I had to pack up our home and find a new place to live. I started with Jayden's room because I knew it was going to take the longest. Touching every single one of his belongings and deciding whether to keep it, donate it, or throw it away was excruciating. I wasn't ready for this. Why was I being forced to do something I wasn't ready for, yet again? I'd had a well-thought-out plan. I was going to stay there one more year, cleaning out every room slowly. Then, I would move to a one-bedroom apartment.

My apartment search quickly became an intense hunt, knowing my thirty days were going to run out. Why was it so hard to find a one-bedroom apartment with a dining room and a storage closet? I was down sizing without a lot of time to get rid of things. Did I mention I wasn't ready? It was more than just limited physical time to prepare; it was limited emotional time to process. Almost every box I packed had some tears in it.

I finally found two apartments that fit my needs. One was 1.5 miles up the road, and the other was in another city about twenty minutes away. My prayer was to not have to move far. I was willing to move, knowing God had somehow arranged this dramatic event to get me out of my comfort zone, but I didn't want to have to change everything about my routines. I wanted to still be close to work and shop at the same grocery store. It wasn't just the home that had memories but our neighborhood and city, too.

God answered my prayers. I was instantly approved for the apartment 1.5 miles up the road. Coincidentally, the apartment complex was one Jayden and I had looked at when we first moved to the area. At that time, it was out of my budget, but now it was about to save me some money. I felt good about the place, knowing Jayden had been there before.

Moving day came, and my girls showed up. I didn't need their help to move; my mom had secured the movers for me. But I needed them to be there for me, emotionally. I had no idea what to expect. Was I going to be frozen, unable to leave the place I last hugged my boy? This was where he last slept and where we laughed and ate together. Was I going to lose it and not be able to talk with the movers? Was I going to punch a hole in the wall? There was no telling.

Before I knew it, everything was in the truck, and we were heading to my new place. I was all settled within three days. Every box was unpacked and broken down. Every room was set up with the decor on the walls. Everything had its place. This was my first apartment by myself, but in some unexplainable way I felt Jayden's presence.

My boy was not far from me no matter where I went. I could go halfway around the world and feel him. He is not gone in some far out universe but with me, inside me, my heart, my soul. There is so much for us to learn about love and eternity. We have barely scratched the surface.

When the one-year anniversary came around, I treated it as if it were his first birthday in heaven rather than his first year gone. This made all the difference for me. Some friends joined me at his grave. We laughed. We cried. We ate pizza.

Jayden Xavier Simmons is healed.

We have every reason to celebrate.

Because when Jayden saw Jesus for the first time, I know he *ran* to Him.

JOURNAL PROMPTS

CHAPTER 1

Describe a specific turning point in your life when the noise of the world became louder than God's voice, drawing you away from Him.

CHAPTER 2

What are some of the struggles from your past that have shaped and refined you?

CHAPTER 3

Was there ever a time when you felt compelled to advocate for someone?

CHAPTER 4

Have you ever had a "Spiritual Year?" If so, write about it. If not, brainstorm what that might look like for you.

CHAPTER 5

What are your feelings about tithing? Do you trust God to do more with the 90% than you could do with the 100%?

CHAPTER 6

Write about a time when your faith was weak, and God showed up in a mighty way.

CHAPTER 7

Around what age did you realize it was time to start making more spiritually-mature decisions? Why then?

CHAPTER 8

When life just keeps knocking you down, what are your tendencies? Do you tend to shut down or lash out? Do you tend to run to God or away from Him?

CHAPTER 9

Do you remember a time when you prayed desperate prayers? Write about it.

CHAPTER 10

Do you know someone whose light shines bright, changing everyone they come in contact with? Describe that person. Consider writing them a letter.

CHAPTER 11

Was there ever a time when you were plagued with guilt because you thought you should have known better? Write yourself an apology note.

CHAPTER 12

How has the devil tried to over play his cards in your life?

CHAPTER 13

Who do you know that has determination like no other? What do you love about them?

CHAPTER 14

If you were given two weeks to live, how would you spend it?

CHAPTER 15

Have a Selah moment—a moment to pause and take a breath. Write whatever you are feeling.

CHAPTER 16

How did you end up meeting grief?

CHAPTER 17

Do you know your why for your life?

CHAPTER 18

How have you coped with grief?

CHAPTER 19

Is there a moment in your life God didn't turn it around and you walked through suffering? Write about it. Have you forgiven God for it?

CHAPTER 20

How has God pursued you throughout your life?

CHAPTER 21

What is your life's mission?

CHAPTER 22

How has life on earth taught you about eternity and love?

RESOURCES

This page contains resources I personally used during my son's battle.

SOCIAL WORKER

Most Children's Hospitals will have a social worker on staff. They will be your greatest resource. Many charities require the social worker to fill out forms and applications for assistance.

HOPEKIDS

HopeKids provides ongoing events, activities, and a powerful, unique support community for families who have a child with cancer or another life-threatening medical condition. They surround these remarkable children and their families with the message that hope is a powerful medicine. They also provide an extensive resource page on their website.
www.hopekids.org

HEROES FOR CHILDREN

Heroes for Children advocates for and provides financial and social assistance to families with children (0 to 22 years old) fighting cancer. No family with a child battling cancer will fight alone.
www.heroesforchildren.org

THE ANDREW MCDONOUGH B+ FOUNDATION

The B+ Foundation has four areas of focus: financial assistance, childhood cancer research, awareness and spreading positivity.

www.bepositive.org

OSTEOSARCOMA INSTITUTE

OSI Connect is a free, easy-to-use resource dedicated to supporting osteosarcoma patients and their families. They connect those affected by the devastating disease with expert physicians to answer questions about all aspects of osteosarcoma, including treatment, possible side effects, and advice for getting the most out of patient visits with their treating physician. They are also well connected with various charitable organizations.

www.osinst.org

NATIONAL CHILDREN'S CANCER SOCIETY

NCCS provides vital and unique services for children with cancer, their families, and survivors. Our comprehensive programs support children and their families at every stage of their journey, addressing immediate and long-term needs, from diagnosis and treatment to survivorship and beyond.

www.thenccs.org

ALEX'S LEMONADE STAND FOUNDATION

ALSF strives to change the lives of children with cancer through funding impactful research, raising awareness, supporting families and empowering everyone to help cure childhood cancer. They also provide an extensive resource page on their website.

www.alexslemonade.org

ACKNOWLEDGMENTS

FIRST AND FOREMOST, I want to thank my family, friends, and church family for their unwavering love, kindness, and generosity throughout our five-year battle and my ongoing journey through grief. Your support carried me in ways words can't fully express. I am deeply grateful to the incredible staff at Medical City Children's Hospital in Dallas for not only treating my son's medical condition with excellence but also welcoming us into the oncology family with compassion and care. A special thank-you to Heroes for Children and HopeKids for being a vital part of our support system—both financially and emotionally. Your presence brought light and joy during some of our hardest days. And finally, thank you to everyone who prayed and spent time helping make Jayden's short but extraordinary life so beautifully memorable.

Find Ashley

Ashley wants to connect with you! Find her on Instagram or Facebook. She shares hope-filled reflections on faith, grief, and healing. Together, we'll find beauty in broken places, celebrate small victories, and discover how God's love carries us through even the hardest seasons.

 @ashley.selby.karney **f** Ashley Selby-Karney

Jayden!

 @leaveyourmarkco